The Autism Spectrum and Further Education

The Autism Spectrum and Further Education
A Guide to Good Practice

Christine Breakey

Jessica Kingsley Publishers
London and Philadelphia

First published in 2006
by Jessica Kingsley Publishers
116 Pentonville Road
London N1 9JB, UK
and
400 Market Street, Suite 400
Philadelphia, PA 19106, USA

www.jkp.com

Library of Congress Cataloging in Publication Data
Breakey, Christine, 1952-
  The autism spectrum and further education : a guide to good practice / Christine Breakey.
    p. cm.
  Includes bibliographical references and index.
  ISBN-13: 978-1-84310-382-0 (pbk. : alk. paper)
  ISBN-10: 1-84310-382-6 (pbk. : alk. paper) 1. Autistic youth--Education (Higher) 2.
Asperger's syndrome--Patients--Education (Higher) I. Title.
  LC4717.5.B74 2006
  371.94--dc22

                                                          2006011506

British Library Cataloguing in Publication Data
A CIP catalogue record for this book is available from the British Library

ISBN-13: 978 1 84310 382 0
ISBN-10: 1 84310 382 6

Printed and bound in Great Britain by
Athenaeum Press, Gateshead, Tyne and Wear

*For my father, who taught me that everyone is equal,
and my mother who 'doesn't have a sense of humour'.*

Contents

Preface

Language is a fascination of mine. It is an extremely powerful tool and has the ability to change what people think. We use language to persuade and to influence people, as well as to describe to explain and to inform. The English language has been influenced by many other languages and as a result gives us a rich choice of vocabulary. Because of this we often have a range of words from which we can choose one which suits our purpose best. Words denote meaning, but they also carry connotations, which imply or suggest additional meaning. The word 'red' for example denotes colour, but the connotations of red are 'danger', 'hot', or 'sexy'. Some connotations are positive, some are negative, and through their connotations, our choice of the words and the way we use language influences our perceptions of people and things. Because of this, I believe that we have a responsibility to use language very carefully and if we are serious about inclusion and equality, then we have a responsibility to ensure that we use language in a way which promotes that. This is not about being politically correct in our language use, as correctness without conviction is almost worthless. It is about using language in a way which does not exclude or marginalize people. It is about using 'inclusive language'. Because of this, I have chosen to use the following terms throughout this book:

Autism

I have used this term frequently to refer to the autism spectrum. When it is used to refer to a particular type of autism, then it is clarified by the prefix 'classic' or 'Kanner's'.

Autistic people

I recognize that the use of this term is controversial, but increasingly, autistic people are telling us that this is how they want to be addressed because they do not experience their autism as something which is additional to them. My generation was taught that it is important to put the people before the disability, so it is difficult for me. The argument from autistic people is very strong and so for the first time, I have chosen to use this term.

Autism spectrum

I have used this term as opposed to autistic spectrum because I consider it to be more correct. Autism is a spectrum condition as opposed to the spectrum being autistic.

Autism spectrum condition

I have chosen to use this term instead of autism spectrum disorder, because autistic people are telling us that they do not want to have the negative connotations of having or being 'disordered'. 'Condition' is their preferred choice and is a more positive term.

Autism specific

I have used this term to indicate something which is based in theoretical and practical knowledge of autism and the individual autistic person. When it is used in the text, the meaning is usually given.

Challenging behaviour

This is a term which I have chosen not to use because of the negative connotations which surround it. The explanation for this is given in the introduction.

Fascination

For a long time, I have disliked the negative connotations that are linked to the word 'obsession' and have sought to use other terms like 'special interest'. I heard Luke Jackson refer to his 'fascinations' and liked it, so I have chosen to use this instead of obsession.

AS

Where this abbreviation occurs, it stands for Asperger syndrome.

He

I have tried to avoid the use of this in its generic form for reasons of gender equality and to avoid the misconception that autism is a purely male condition. I find the use of the alternative s/he clumsy so have preferred the term 'autistic people', unless specifically referring to males.

ASC

Where this abbreviation is used it stands for autism spectrum condition.

All other abbreviations are explained in the text.

Introduction

Autism is one of the most fascinating and intriguing conditions which we encounter. It challenges our assumptions about everything which we take for granted in our daily lives and forces us to recognize and question our own prejudices and preconceptions. Over the last 20 or so years, our understanding of the condition has progressed in leaps and bounds. There are now numerous books written on the subject, and in the last decade it has become possible to study autism at undergraduate and postgraduate levels. Training courses abound and there is no shortage of candidates who want to extend their knowledge, skills and practice. Despite this availability of study and literature, we still know relatively little about autism. This is because interesting and fascinating though it may be as an area of study, autism is much, much more than this. *Autism is a reality.*

It is a state of being which only autistic people can experience and truly know. Traditionally, autistic people have been viewed as contributing useful 'insights' and 'experience' into the academic arena, but they have not been sufficiently recognized in the intellectual discussions and exploration of the condition. I believe that this is now changing and autistic people are beginning to shout from the roof tops. We neuro-typical people, if we really want to learn more about autism, must listen to what they are telling us.

If we listen to what autistic people tell us, we begin to realize that our progress in terms of knowledge and understanding has been slow, because we have started from the wrong position. We have started from the outside of the condition and focused on the symptoms (that is the behaviour), instead of from the inside and focused on what autistic people are, or how their differences result in the so-called stereotypical behaviours which we associate with autism. In line with this, we have viewed autism as a problem within the person, which must be treated, cured or modified. So, we search for solutions which enable the autistic person to modify their behaviour and 'pretend to be normal'. This is a state which they can never achieve, because they are autistic, whatever they may appear to be. As a result, we have become very successful in diagnosing autism, but far less successful in reaching and communicating with autistic people. Despite our efforts, there are still relatively few autistic people who are able to survive successfully the challenges of university and the world of employment, despite their cognitive ability, and there are significantly more who experience anxiety and depression as a consequence.

I have written this book for two reasons. First, as someone who is an avid reader and student in the field of autism, and as a professional who was given the responsibility in 1999, for setting up an autism specialist support service in a Further Education (FE) college, I discovered that very little was written to guide my practice. This book is an attempt to do that for the many more FE practitioners who are now working with autistic people. The second reason is more of a 'mission' to challenge current attitudes towards autistic people. If we are truly serious about inclusion, then we must alter the way we view autism and give autistic people the recognition for their experience and expertise. We must stop viewing them and their autism as a problem and we must search for solutions to their impairments within society, instead of within them. This book also attempts to encourage people to do this.

I would not want to give the impression that I do not value academic theory. I believe firmly that our practice must be grounded in tried and tested academic theory and practice. However, I also believe that autistic people must be given their right of place as 'experts' in this field. Because of this, I have attempted to always put the theories, views and opinions of autistic people first, but I have also included theories which I consider essential to underpinning our current knowledge and practice. When I have been theoretical, I have tried to make the theories accessible and easy to read.

There is no chapter on 'challenging behaviour'. This is because I choose not to use this term, preferring to think that there is no such thing. I don't view behaviour as something which we have, which the common usage of the term 'challenging behaviour' has come to mean. Neither do I view behaviour as something which we are as in the term 'well behaved'. I view behaviour as something which we do. Whether it is viewed as 'challenging' depends on the feelings, interpretations and reactions of others. From my point of view, autistic people's behaviours aren't in themselves 'challenging'. They are an expression of their autism and of the challenges which autistic people face living in a neuro-typical world. As such they are a means of communication and they tell us something. The challenge for me is to not only listen but to understand. The label of autism is something which we give to people based on what we see of their outward behaviour, whilst this 'thing' called autism is something internal to the person. Because of this, I have chosen to focus on how autistic people think and learn, rather than how they behave.

This book is intended to give practical guidance to FE practitioners, but I think that it could be used by parents and carers of autistic people, who want to know what to look for in a Post-16 provision for autistic people. The personal accounts might be of particular interest to parents and it is my hope that they will inspire others to be confident in challenging a system which does not fit everyone.

This is not an academic book but is written from my own experience. Everything which is suggested in here has been tried and tested and has 'worked'. The examples which are used are real, but I have changed some names for reasons of confidentiality. I agonized over my decision to include personal accounts, but have chosen to include them because I think that they are inspirational and because personal testimony is far more powerful than anything I might have to say.

I hope more than anything that it will be of use.

CHAPTER 1

Breaking Down Barriers

Background

There is no doubt that autistic people are excluded from many social activities which many neuro-typical people would see as fundamental human rights. We talk about the 'right to work' or the 'right to an education' yet the National Autistic Society estimated in 2001 that only 6 per cent of autistic people are in full-time employment and that the school exclusion rate for autistic children is more than 20 times the national average (Barnard *et al.* 2001). A National Autistic Society (NAS) survey in 2000 found that only 8 per cent of autistic people are in a long-term sexual relationship and that although there are no accurate figures available, it is known that there are significantly higher numbers of autistic people who attempt suicide (Barnard *et al.* 2000). Personal experience has demonstrated that in some instances, autistic people are denied access to basic health and hospital services, and that people who have a diagnosis of Asperger syndrome are inadequately supported, or even not supported, at Further Education colleges and universities. I have known autistic people to be labelled as 'habitual complainants' or 'too challenging', or even 'too different', and as a result denied access to the very public services which are designed to support them. I do not believe that this is the fault of the individuals who work in these services. Rather, it is the logical conclusion generated by a dominant societal view of autism, which seeks to 'cure' and to 'normalize'. When 'cure' and 'normalization' is not achieved, then the autistic person is blamed for such things as 'failure to comply', 'unwillingness to engage', 'being too difficult' or 'lack of conformity'.

On a personal level autistic people are continually denied the social contact, interactions and relationships which many of us would describe as 'fundamental to our existence'. They are marginalized and misunderstood and are often misrepresented, even by ASC specialists, who help to perpetuate the myth that autistic people are 'unable to empathize', 'lack emotions', 'don't have any imagination', or 'cannot cope with change or make choices' etc. The result of this 'lack of' model or understanding of autism is that autistic people are seen as 'less than' whole, and are often denied opportunities to access and participate in everyday life experiences, either with, or without support. Most neuro-typical people have consequently never had the opportunity to expose these myths which surround autistic people and to discover that autistic people may not have difficulties experiencing any of these 'stereotypical features', but rather they express these intense feelings and emotions in a way which we, neuro-typical people fail to recognize, or find 'inappropriate'.

With very few exceptions such as A.S. Neil's Summerhill, most educational establishments require a certain degree of conformity to the status quo. In fact, it could be argued that in schools such as Summerhill, students are still expected to conform with the status quo, but to a status quo which is specific to the culture and society of the school, although non-conventional in terms of the wider or host society in which it exists. For many autistic people, the notion of conformity is a minefield, beset with unwritten rules and conventions, which everyone else knows and understands, but no one shares. Because of this, few autistic adults I have worked with describe their educational experiences positively, regardless of whether those experiences have been in the special school or mainstream sector. Many, particularly those who have been diagnosed as having Asperger syndrome say that they have been bullied somewhere along the way. Most alarmingly, this has not always been by their peers. Many say that they have suffered humiliation at the hands of people who are in authority over them, and many say that they have been blamed for initiating the bullying. Temple Grandin gives an example of what might be termed 'professional bullying', when she describes a governess who was aware of her hyper-sensitivity to sound, and used this as a means of controlling and punishing her behaviour (Grandin and

Scariano 1986, p.19). This was in the 1950s and our increased knowl-edge and awareness of autism should have improved our practice since then, but unfortunately my experience supports the view that autistic people still experience bullying at the hands of professionals and peers alike. Mostly, the bullying is subtle and is often justified as 'teas-ing'. Frequently these subtle forms of bullying present very real barri-ers to the autistic person's access to education.

There is a myth which suggests that autistic people experience more bullying at school than they do in the FE environment. I wish this was the case. It is my experience that the FE environment attempts to actively engage students in being responsible for their own learning by claiming to treat them as adults and in return expects them to behave as adults. This expectation is unrealistic for many 16-year-olds to achieve, and many struggle without the structure and support that they were used to at school. This expectation to 'be adult', to be 'responsible for one's own learning', 'to make one's own decisions' etc, which is encouraged but rarely actively taught at col-lege, often leads to increased vulnerability for many students but par-ticularly for autistic people. It also leads to increased opportunities, albeit more subtle, for the bullies. The bullying is then often rendered invisible by the fostering of independence and lack of supervision, which is part of the FE ethos. Often, such incidents are only brought to light when the autistic person responds to the bullying in a way which is seen as 'socially unacceptable'. In situations like this, lack of specialist knowledge of ASC usually means that the autistic person has no one to negotiate on their behalf, or explain their reasons for their behaviour. Despite the fact that they have disclosed their dis-ability, and the requirement that 'reasonable adjustments' be made, they are consequently blamed and subsequently punished for their response. This can be seen in the following example:

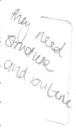

Example 1: James

James who has a diagnosis of high functioning autism is sup-ported by a learner support assistant (LSA), in his Maths class. He is hyper-sensitive to sound and one of his peers, John, is aware that he can be easily 'wound up' by the sound of a pencil tapping on the desk. John finds it amusing to sit next to James, tap his pencil and wait for the reaction. James is unable to filter out the sound and finds it increasingly difficult to concentrate on his work. He starts fidgeting and muttering under his breath. John finds this amusing and makes eye contact with James, makes faces at him and laughs, when the LSA is looking somewhere else, upsetting James further. Unaware of the full situation, the LSA attempts to use humour to stop James from muttering and swearing under his breath. Very quickly, James is unable to cope with the situation. He pushes his desk away from him, inadvertently pushing it into the girl who is sitting in front of him and hurting her back. He storms out of the room in a rage, swearing and kicking doors along the way. He kicks a hole in one of the doors, which upsets him even more, so he picks up a chair and throws it. This hits the ceiling and breaks one of the lights. He storms out of the building with the LSA following, trying to reason with him. He eventually calms down after a half hour brisk walk away from the college. As a result of this, he is subject to the college disciplinary procedure and is suspended from college for two weeks. His lecturers report that he is 'difficult to manage, unreasonable and volatile'.

Student is not being understood, retaliates bully and gets blamed.   *lack of understanding*

I have chosen this example which describes a situation that is not unusual. It demonstrates how lack of understanding of ASC leads to discrimination at individual and institutional levels, to the point where the barriers which the autistic person faces are so great that they are denied access and are excluded from mainstream institutions. It is my belief that autistic people continue to be excluded from many areas of social activities, including FE, when other disabled people such as those with physical impairments have made breakthroughs. This is not through any 'fault' or 'impairment' on the part of autistic people, but because of the social barriers which act against them. These social barriers create situations where the autistic person is so challenged by an over-stimulating and high arousal environment that they have no alternative but to use whatever coping strategies which

could this be a focus

environment

larger Other disabilities are no
stereo typed full look
of awareness
for autistic

are available to them, to deal with the situation in hand. In extreme cases, this may result in a complete 'overload' of the senses, which some autistic people call 'melt down', as in the example described above. In other instances, the autistic person may resort to other familiar strategies for coping such as hand flapping, talking to themselves, or self-harming. These behaviours are then taken to reinforce and perpetuate the stereotypical view of autism as 'challenging'. In other areas, such as race, gender and physical disabilities, the negative implications of stereotyping and their influence on prejudice and discrimination have been recognized and well explored. We must ask therefore why the dominant view of autism is still so stereotypical. It is my view that this is linked to our understanding of the nature of autism as a condition, but more importantly it is linked to the way that neuro-typical people have traditionally found solutions to it.

Unlike some other areas of disability, autism is primarily a social condition and affects all areas of communication. (This is discussed in more detail within a theoretical framework, in later chapters.) Because of this, like dyslexia, and dyspraxia, to name but two conditions, autism is often termed a 'hidden disability'. Autistic people tell us that they are given many labels, by their neuro-typical peers. Typically these are: 'odd'; strange; 'weird'; 'eccentric'; 'badly behaved', 'nerdy; or 'freaks' and 'geeks' (Jackson 2002). At best, autistic people are termed 'different'. It is not the aim of this book to explore social theories on topics such as stereotyping, prejudice and discrimination. It may be that we are pack animals by nature and group together because of this, or it may be that psychologically we are threatened by anything which is outside of our frame of reference for 'similar', or our 'comfort zone'. We may not really know why we discriminate in this way. Whatever the reason for our prejudice and discrimination, it is enough for the purpose of this chapter, to just acknowledge their existence and to leave the exploration of reason for those attitudes and behaviours to other writers and other books. So, for whatever reason, we seem to be programmed as human beings to dislike 'difference' in others, but we do not dislike all differences. We only seem to dislike difference when it reaches a significant level. We can tolerate some difference up to a point, but there does come a point where that difference becomes too different to sit comfortably within our

'we only dislike differences when they reach a significant level'

frame of reference and the different person is no longer seen as eccentric, but takes on the more negative stereotypical labels listed above. There is a perception that this is less likely to happen to physically disabled people, particularly if their communication is not impaired, because mainstream society is more able to identify and sympathize with their situation. I'm not sure if this is an accurate perception, but it does seem that autism, because it affects social interactions and is not obvious, is more difficult for people to recognize, accept and understand.

Stereotyping, prejudice and discrimination are attitudinal reasons why autistic people experience such high levels of exclusion within society. I believe that these attitudes and beliefs are encouraged and fed by an outdated academic and medical view of autism which seems to blame the autistic person for whatever way their autism manifests itself. In this way, the barriers to inclusion for autistic people have been seen to be located within the person themselves and almost by default, the removal of those barriers has become the responsibility of the autistic person. In this way, wider society has managed to ignore the societal barriers which define this particular disability and exclude autistic people. This view is supported by autistic people who have written about their experience. Wendy Lawson, writes: 'I do not experience my autism as being "disordered" or "impaired" so much as I experience it as being "disabled" in a world that doesn't understand autism' (Lawson 2001, p.12).

Donna Williams, also an autistic woman describes the many barriers which autistic people face within education as 'sources of aversion' and states that aversion is a 'repelling force' (Williams 1996, p.284). As well as neuro-typical attitudes and beliefs, she lists many environmental conditions which present as barriers for autistic people. Traditionally, autistic people's views, if they have not proven themselves first as academics, have been thought interesting in terms of biographical insights, but have not always been taken very seriously in terms of 'knowledge'. However, there is now a wealth of academic knowledge and research, which also supports this view. Why then have these issues not been addressed?

The medical model of disability versus the social model of disability

Occasionally it has happened that when I speak at training sessions or conferences, someone, invariably male, will come to talk to me afterwards to say that they have identified with what I have talked about and that they think that they may have Asperger syndrome. Usually, they have a sense of relief that they have eventually identified what they have been aware of as a life-long 'difference'. Often they ask me where and how they can obtain a diagnosis. As ASC is a medical diagnosis, usually made by a psychiatrist, I refer them in the first instance, to their GP. More often than not, as autism, more particularly Asperger syndrome, is still a relatively recent diagnostic category, their GP is not very aware of the condition, and will then contact me for further advice. Despite this lack of awareness and knowledge, autism remains a medical diagnosis and is firmly in the medical domain. Perhaps because of this, it has traditionally been, and is still understood through the 'medical model' of disability.

The medical model views disability almost wholly in terms of individuals and their impairments and focuses on this as a 'problem'. Having identified the 'problem', it then locates it within the individual and seeks to cure or compensate for what is 'wrong' with them. Locating the 'problem' within the individual in this way leads to a particular way of viewing disability which defines disabled people in terms of what they can't do, in other words, their physical, sensory or intellectual deficits. What disabled people can't do is then measured against the 'norm' as defined by the 'able-bodied' world. This definition of disability and disabled people then leads to solutions which are also located within the individual. In terms of autistic people, this is often expressed in the need for medication and the requirement for their outward behaviour to conform, or be socially 'acceptable' or 'appropriate', regardless of the reasons for their behaviour or how they are feeling. The success of this model is then measured in terms of how far the autistic person is able to accommodate themselves to living as 'normally' as possible with the 'disadvantage' of having autism. There is no doubt that some autistic people have survived this process of 'pretending to be normal' and have achieved in line with their potential, but at what cost? Liane Holliday Willey is one example of the success of this model. She has documented her journey to where she is now 'a point that sits balanced between neurologically typical and Asperger syndrome' beautifully, and is happy. Despite this she writes:

> In other ways, I meet who I am with a certain amount of sadness, for I often wonder what parts of me I had to leave behind before I came to this place in my life. Would I have been a better writer if I had allowed my skewed take to find its way to paper? Was there a wonderfully quirky and surreal book hidden beneath my idiosyncrasies that will now never be found because I can bridle so many of my old habits and thinking patterns? If I had not been taught and encouraged to be as social as I now am, would I have found a different but somehow more satisfying kind of individualized lifestyle? Would I have avoided my irritable bowel syndrome and panic attacks, if I had not tried so hard to pretend to be normal? (Willey 1999, p.120)

The cost to her clearly has been great. For some autistic people, it can be too great and this is reflected in the high numbers of autistic people, particularly those diagnosed with Asperger syndrome, who experience mental health problems.

If we continue to view autism through the medical model, we fail to search for solutions beyond the person themselves and we fail to address the root cause of the disadvantages which autistic people experience. If we do this, then all we as neuro-typical people can offer is 'help' for the autistic person to cope with the negative message that they are constantly given, that they are less than 'normal'. I believe that if this is all that we do, we are failing in our duty and responsibility as human beings.

There is an alternative way of viewing autism which some autistic people are championing. In the 1970s, the British Disability Movement challenged the dominant medical model of disability and proposed an alternative model – the social model. Defining this model has not been without its difficulties, but a recent definition is as follows:

The social model of disability represents nothing more complicated than a focus on the economic, environmental and cultural barriers encountered by people viewed by others as having some form of impairment. These include inaccessible education, information and communication systems, working environments, inadequate disability benefits, discriminatory health and social support services, inaccessible transport, houses and public buildings and amenities and the devaluing of disabled people through negative images of the media – films, television and newspapers. (Barnes 2003, p.346)

The social model of disability has been put forward by disabled people who feel that the medical model does not provide an adequate explanation for the exclusion which they experience from mainstream society. They argue that the 'problems' which they experience are not caused by their impairments, but by the way in which society is organized. Because of this, the social model makes the important distinction between 'impairment' and 'disability'. According to the social model, impairment refers to a lack of something which would ordinarily be expected to be there. This can be physical or cognitive, and the absence of it limits the person's ability to function. Disability on the other hand refers to the disadvantages, restrictions and exclusion which a person experiences from social organizations which fail to take account of their impairments. This clearly shows that disability is caused and defined by societal barriers which take little or no account of people who have impairments, and which prevent disabled people from participating in social, cultural and economic life. These barriers are then reflected in society's attitudes so that disabled people become objects of pity, or are perceived in negative and discriminatory ways. If the problems which disabled people experience are directly caused by the barriers within society, then it follows that the solutions for these problems lie in the removal of those barriers. If disabled people are therefore to be included within mainstream society, then the way society is organized has to be changed. According to this model, this in turn will have a positive effect on attitudes towards disabled people. We all have a responsibility therefore to break these barriers down.

For some reason, autistic people have until very recently been absent from this debate. It may be because the nature of the condition has lead to the mistaken and patriarchal belief that autistic people are dependent on their neuro-typical parents and professionals to know what is best for them and to speak on their behalf. Whatever the reason, things are now changing and autistic people are asserting themselves and are speaking into the debate. Some neuro-typical people have been challenged by this and are supporting them.

Implications for autistic people

Viewing autism through the social model challenges the dominant view of autism. It shifts the focus from the individual and locates the 'problem' within society and its organizations. According to this model, autistic people are no longer viewed as 'problematic' or 'challenging' but as experiencing problems or difficulties which are caused and challenged by society's lack of provision and the creation of barriers within society. This model challenges the prejudice and discrimination which autistic people experience on a daily basis and leads to a fundamental need to shift our professional focus and approach from one which seeks to normalize and teach the autistic person to 'pretend to be normal', to one which examines and addresses the barriers in the organizations in which we work, so that they become more accessible and inclusive for autistic people.

There is a negative implication of the social model, which I have experienced and which I feel is worth mentioning. People often ask me if when autistic people learn more about their autism, it leads to them in some way trying to take advantage of being autistic. I often ask these people if they have a particular talent, and if they have, do they use it to their advantage. But that is really facetious of me, because I do understand what they mean. It has never been my experience that autistic people use their autism to gain unfair advantage over their neuro-typical peers. However, on one occasion I have known someone misunderstand and misinterpret the social model of disability and apply it very rigidly to their own situation. This led to them believing that they had no personal responsibility for their actions, and that the 'law of the land' was one of society's barriers, *one one of someone who was autistic thought they could break the law*

which should be removed. The logical conclusion of this was that they should be allowed to break the law because of their impairment. I do not want to imply that this happened because the person concerned was autistic, as there were many other factors which may have contributed to this situation. I am also well aware that neuro-typical people also regularly misinterpret, manipulate and misapply the law to their own advantage. I use it only as an example to demonstrate how the social model, (along with many other theoretical models) can be misused. There is sometimes a dilemma though in applying the social model rigidly to autism. Autism is the label which we give to something which is essentially internal to the autistic person. What we observe, are the strategies which the autistic person employs to enable them to cope in a world which is continuously at odds with their autism. Because we cannot see and experience what is an internal reality for the autistic person, we label the 'observable' as the condition. In this way, we define autism as a social condition which affects communication and social interactions. This primarily means 'social behaviour'. Our behaviour is something we all have to manage, monitor and control, all of the time. It is affected by outside conditions, but ultimately, we are expected to take full responsibility for our own actions. Because of this, it is argued that it is not always possible to effectively remove all societal barriers which affect all autistic people, particularly because of the unique and individual nature of the condition. When this is argued, then the onus is once again put onto the autistic person to 'fit in' and conform, to some degree. This means, to 'act normal'. Conformity is always an extremely controversial area which is accompanied by massive ethical dilemmas (see Chapter 7), but it is something which we are all expected to do, in every situation which we experience, without being aware of it. Autistic 'normality' however is quite different to neuro-typical 'normality' and what we are actually asking the autistic person to do is to conform to neuro-typical 'normality'. Clearly, this is a situation which cannot be resolved easily and there is a need for greater understanding and flexibility. The real danger is that when neuro-typical people are confronted by barriers which appear insurmountable, they are sometimes defeated and the result is that they do not attempt to remove the barriers which can more readily be removed.

We are exp to take full responsibility for our own actions, we au have to manage and control. It is not always possible

Supports my theory.

We are asking them to conform.

According to the social model, barriers which disable autistic people can be:

- Prejudice, stereotypes and discrimination.

- Inflexible organizational procedures and practices.

- Inaccessible information.

- Inaccessible buildings.

- Inaccessible transport.

It is not difficult to identify barriers within FE for autistic people in all of these areas.

Identifying the barriers

1. Prejudice, stereotypes and discrimination

I have already mentioned that the FE environment can inadvertently foster and fail to recognize the existence of these attitudes and practices. I have also touched on how these attitudes lead to bullying. Autistic people report time and time again of being on the receiving end of negative attitudes and discrimination. Kevin Phillips, gives an incredible factual account of the negative attitudes and bullying he was subjected to which finally led to him being suspended from school. On Thursday 5 April 1990, he finally snapped and got into a fight with one of the bullies. Both he and the bully were suspended. On the surface, this appears to be a fair and reasonable judgement on behalf of the school, as violence cannot be tolerated and has to be seen to be taken seriously. Kevin explains the injustice of it in the following example from his website:

Example 2: Kevin

Before you go away thinking I am an out of control thug and need anger management lessons, it is worth stating that in the months before this happened, the person I fought with had hit me full whack on the forehead with a chair leg which went 3 cm above my left eye. If it had connected in my eye I could have been blinded for life. It is worth remembering that in the weeks before our joint suspension, he sat behind me in an exam and pulled my chair back with the chair legs and told me to sit down and placed lard on my chair, so I got it all over my trousers. He tipped my work into a bin. As well as the punch-up he had with me, he was also suspended several other times for other incidents. He would be OK for spells of time but could have an unpredictable and violent temper at other times. This combined with the fact that something had probably snapped in his mind that day, and the fact that to many people at the time I was perceived as someone who could be annoying and weird, had largely caused the fight. Maybe something had happened that morning that was unrelated to school, unrelated to me or anyone else in school, that had annoyed or upset him, and this was his way of venting rage. Who knows?

How many times I can't remember but I know he was put on report on numerous occasions and even in the isolation unit of the School. He tried to pick a fight with me on Monday 12 June 1989. That afternoon there was a fight with two other boys in my class in the dinner queue, totally unconnected with either me or him. At home time that day, he decided he wanted a 'fight with someone' because 'there had been a fight earlier that day and I had felt left out'. He lunged at me but before he could do so he was stopped by two teachers, one of whom taught science and was Scottish. There was a joke going around school that he had a helicopter!

His behaviour was fine in the final year. He totally changed. It is also wrong to single him out because there were others like him in that secondary school and worse. I am not singling him for any personal reasons. Had I been involved in a fight with anyone else in the year and it had led to my suspension, I would have wrote about them instead of him.

I wish we both would have been expelled. It would have been the best thing that could have happened to me and it would have been for him.

(Kevin Phillips, www.angelfire.com, reproduced with permission)

equality
Act -
professionals
should be
educated in
" Equal opps"

Clearly, lack of awareness of autism and a failure to address the discrimination which Kevin experienced throughout his school life led to his exclusion, albeit a temporary one. Again, this was over ten years ago and we are now better informed about prejudice and discrimination. All professionals should have been educated in terms of 'equal opportunities', 'inclusion' and 'disabled people's rights'. Laws have been updated, so surely things must be different now? This however, does not seem to be the case. Attitudes of stereotyping, prejudice and discrimination towards autistic people still lead to the type of behaviour which Kevin experienced in 1990, and present very real barriers for autistic people.

Luke Jackson talks very eloquently about his experience of being bullied 'All of my life' (Jackson 2002, p.135). Luke was only 13 at the time of writing this, and had not experienced FE, but there is no evidence to support the view that it would have been any different from school. Speaking at a conference at King Ecgbert's School in Sheffield, in July 2004, Luke informed his audience that he is now home educated and is following an Open University degree because school had become intolerable for him. In effect, he has been excluded by the stereotypical views of others who see him as a 'freak', 'geek' and 'nerd'. He has been on the receiving end of prejudice and discrimination, and it has been intolerable.

These are only two examples but experience shows that there are many more. FE colleges are not always good at identifying the need for support at interview, and there are many autistic people who have not gained access to FE because of this. The minefield known as 'interviewing technique' is, without specific teaching, elusive at the best of times, but for autistic people it can be unfathomable. First impressions, which are inevitably based in both positive and negative stereotypes, by necessity, form the basis of the interviewer's judgement. In this setting, a faux pas by the interviewee, which in other situations is relatively easily rectified, can lead to snap judgements which limit access and lead to exclusion. At best it can result in the view that the autistic person is less academically able than their application suggests. Coupled with this, not all FE lecturers are good interviewers, and as a body, present a broad range of communication skills. The result of this is that many autistic people are misunderstood at interview, and are often

[handwritten: autistic students do courses that are beneath their ability]

encouraged to follow courses which are beneath their ability, or for which they have no interest or motivation. Sometimes, the disclosure of the condition creates anxiety in the minds of interviewers who have no knowledge of the condition and the unfounded decision that the autistic person would present a 'health and safety risk' is made. In this way, despite legislation which is designed to prevent it, autistic people are sometimes excluded from courses for which they are suitably qualified, for no other reason other than they are autistic.

[handwritten margin: Interviewers have no awareness of autism]

It is without doubt that stereotypes, prejudice and discrimination are barriers within FE colleges, which autistic people face on a daily basis. If we are serious about inclusion and equality, then we have a responsibility to remove them.

[handwritten margin: against equality At xoo]

2. Inflexible organizational procedures and practices

There are between 500 and 600 FE colleges in the UK. Most of these are large independent organizations. In the current climate, education has taken on the culture of big business. It is now a competitive industry which has to justify income and expenditure. Of course we must be accountable for how we use society's resources, but to those of us on the ground floor, it does sometimes appear that the focus on people and learning has been lost in the process. Consequently, FE colleges are bureaucratic places, often full of bureaucratic people, especially it seems in management and human resources. A faceless person has ultimate responsibility for proving the quality of the service which students receive and claim forms have to be accurately submitted to generate funding. Evidence has to be given to prove that the work has been completed to a satisfactory standard and inspectors and auditors take over the college for weeks at a time to check that this is so. Payments such as expenses and mileage can appear to be withheld on another faceless person's whim, and there are forms in triplicate, for everything. At times it seems like the organization has an identity of its own and functions purely to satisfy its own needs. Lecturers struggle with ever-increasing deadlines and workloads and can be frequently heard saying that the level of paperwork which they have to do has reached unmanageable proportions. In this culture, it can be difficult to keep sight of what their job is and who

[handwritten margin: FE big business money making scheme]

[handwritten: The tutors have too much paperwork, its hard to keep sight of what their job is]

they are there for and for some, stress has become a daily experience which is reflected in the concern of the lecturers' unions.

Colleges are also stressful places for students. Some colleges are better than others in terms of the additional support and pastoral care which they provide, but however enlightened and progressive these services are within the individual organizations, it is difficult for students' individual needs to be met. Inclusion, as defined by the Tomlinson Report means 'finding the best fit or match between the individual student's learning requirement and the educational provision' (Hesmondhalgh and Breakey 2001, p.191). It is essentially about finding practical solutions to an individual student's learning needs. Practitioners however, often see inclusion as an intellectual ideal which is both impractical and unattainable. I think that this is because inclusion by this definition requires an individual, person-centred approach which can only be achieved within an organization which is flexible in terms of its procedures and practices. As I have described, most FE colleges are large bureaucracies which by their very nature are inflexible. Such organizations do not easily lend themselves to person-centred planning and individual learning programmes, whatever policies are in place. Policies however, are the first step to removing barriers and ensuring equality and excellence. I would not wish to suggest that policies are not important. However, a policy is only as good as the procedures and practice which it generates. If a policy or the implementation of that policy is not flexible enough to result in good practice, then it is only worth the paper it is written on. Policies on inclusion, equality, bullying etc are essential in forming a corporate approach to challenging those areas. However, when we question some policies and practices, they often appear to be for the benefit of the organization, and not the individual. Financial constraints and implications, together with the need to evidence the organization's commitment to their legal obligations can appear to be the main motivator for their existence.

On an everyday basis, it can be seen that many polices lead to practices which serve the organization more than the individuals within it. Teaching staff have little influence over the numbers of students in their classes. Funding is directly linked to student numbers and retention and achievement and a course's viability can depend on these. Timetabling and rooming is subject to efficient use of the building, and does not take lecturers' or students' needs into account. The result is that lecturers frequently have to carry boxes of work long distances and students find it difficult to negotiate rooms in the given time, or have long periods of inactivity between lessons. For neuro-typical people, these things may be inconveniences which irritate and which we moan about and adjust our practice or equipment to accommodate them. For autistic people, they present very real barriers which can make the difference between being able to access college or not. In addition, college procedures and practices are affected by outside organizations' policies, which add yet another dimension to the experience for students and staff. These are often even more bureaucratic and inflexible than the college. This is never more clearly demonstrated than in the area of exam concessions. The policies of the exam boards are 'written in stone', with no flexibility for individuals whatsoever. As a result, autistic candidates who may have profound semantic and pragmatic impairments will not be allowed a reader if their mechanical reading skill is fluent, nor will they be able to have questions translated for them, so that any ambiguities of language and irrelevant context is removed. Once again, barriers are created, which ultimately have the effect of excluding autistic people from succeeding in Further Education.

It may be that some people are 'born teachers' who seem to be naturally gifted in their craft. If this is the case, then I think that these people are few and far between. Most of us come to the profession with some skills, intuition and personality traits which assist us in such areas as relating to our students, or classroom management, but for the vast number of us, teaching is a learnt and practiced art. For the majority of us, 'good practice' is something which we continue to work hard to achieve, despite many years of study and training. This is not made any easier by the difficulty in defining the term 'good practice'.

The notion of what constitutes 'good practice' is problematic for all teachers, whether in the mainstream or special school sectors. Some argue that good practice is related to a level of quality, or excellence which can be inspected and measured. Others argue that it is a minimum standard or 'norm' which should be attained. Either way, 'good practice' equates with 'good teaching'. Whatever definition we prefer, knowledge of how people learn, must be an essential prerequisite for 'good teaching' to take place. As autism impacts on all areas of a person's life, including their thinking and learning, good autism practice must accommodate this. This means that for any practice to be considered 'good' in terms of teaching autistic people, it has to be 'autism specific'.

The term 'autism specific' is worth explaining as practitioners frequently use it without fully understanding what it means. Through misuse, it has been diluted and has come to mean 'influenced by knowledge of autism', whereas in fact, 'autism specific' means much more than that. 'Autism specific' means combining a sound theoretical knowledge of autism with an equally sound knowledge of how autism impacts uniquely on the individual, in terms of their thinking, acting, perceptions, behaviour, communication and experiences. 'Autism specific' then means applying this combined knowledge to the practical task of (in this instance) teaching the autistic person. It is a highly specialized skill and it is not easy. Some people are more intuitive than others, but my experience suggests that even the most intuitive of practitioners require a high level of training and practice to be able to adapt the curriculum and their teaching methods so that they are 'autism specific'. Most practitioners have not experienced this level of specialized training and practice. The impact of this, in terms of support, is that most autistic students do not receive 'autism-specific' support. They receive 'generic' support, which often at its best does not meet their individual needs and which often results in frustration, failure and exclusion. This was highlighted in a report published by the National Autistic Society (Barnard *et al.* 2000), which found that the biggest single group of children who are excluded from school are autistic. The reason given for this, in both the mainstream and special school sectors was the lack of appropriately trained support staff. There is no evidence to suggest that FE practitioners are better trained in this area than school teachers, so it is fair to assume that these figures can be loosely applied to FE. In this way, practice can be clearly identified as a disabling barrier for autistic people.

3. Inaccessible information

Information is disseminated using a variety of media, but the process is essentially the same and is described simply in Figure 1.1.

Figure 1.1: Simple model of communication – one to one

Whatever medium is used to convey a message, it is first of all put into some sort of code by the person who sends it. So, at this stage of the information process, a decision is made to convey the message through words, gesture, picture, song, sign etc. For the message to be received, it has to be understood, which means that it then has to be decoded. If the recipient does not know the code in which the message is sent, then the process is incomplete and it is as effective as if the message has not been sent. In this very simple model (Figure 1.1) which demonstrates one-to-one communication, there is a potential for communication breakdown or miscommunication at two points – the encoding and the decoding stages. In big organizations however, the message may be originally encoded by one person, but it is sent out to hundreds of people. Through the dissemination process, the potential for miscommunication and communication breakdown is multiplied accordingly (see Figure 1.2, in this instance, to 13 potential points).

This very simply demonstrates how difficult effective communication can be in large organizations, and why information may not always be received in the way it was intended, by the people for whom it was intended. However, autism adds another dimension to the process. Autism challenges the suitability of the media which conveys the message.

As already described in this chapter, FE colleges are large bureaucratic organizations which employ large numbers of people and teach even larger numbers of students. Disseminating information effec-

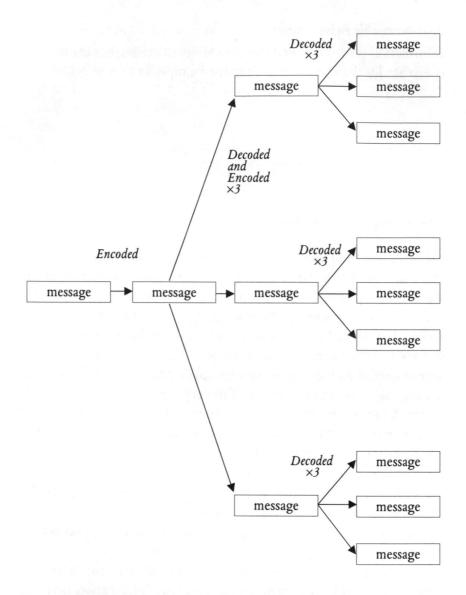

Figure 1.2: Simple model of communication from 1 to 13 people

tively to such large numbers is a difficult process which FE colleges tend to approach via the written and the spoken word. As a result, glossy magazines and brochures are produced which are aimed at attracting potential students. Leaflets and posters are displayed to inform students of the support services which are available for them when they come to college. Websites are set up, which students can access. When there are organizational changes which affect students, memos are sent to tutors, who have the responsibility to pass the information on to their groups. None of this information is delivered in an 'autism-specific way'. As a result, it is not received by the autistic person. The FE ethos views students as adults and expects them to take some share of the responsibility for their own learning. Part of this is that they are expected to ask questions and seek out information for themselves. When there has been a breakdown in the dissemination of information, they are expected to be able to deal with the consequences in an adult way. The experience for neuro-typical people is often frustrating and annoying. For autistic people however, the experience can be devastating. Autistic people receive and process information differently from their neuro-typical peers. It is virtually impossible for them to receive information when the media and the process of disseminating that information are so inappropriate for them. Accessibility to that information is denied and once again, barriers which discriminate against them are set in place.

Example 3: Richard

Richard is sensitive to sound, smell, temperature, touch and light. When he arrives at college, he has to walk through a noisy group of people smoking outside. His English lesson takes place in the room next to the girl's toilets. Throughout the lesson, the muffled sound of doors banging and the hand drier can be heard by everyone. Richard also hears the sound of the toilets being flushed and smells the cleaning products. The room is very hot. There is no air-conditioning and it is impossible to open the windows because there is a football lesson taking place directly outside the window. The strip lighting in the room is flickering and buzzing and the brightly coloured posters on the walls are reflecting the patterns of the sunlight. Richard is wearing shorts and the fabric of the chair's seat scratches his legs. English is a difficult subject for Richard and he is trying hard to concentrate on the task that has been set for him. He is clearly stressed which is demonstrated by him asking repetitive questions, when the fire alarm is tested without warning. It only rings for a few seconds, but Richard is clearly overwhelmed by it. One of his peers notices that he is frightened by this, and makes an attempt to reassure him by putting his arm around his shoulder. Richard is unable to cope, pushes the well-meaning student away, starts shouting, pushing, swearing and crying and eventually runs out of the room. The following week, his English lecturer who has been alarmed by this, suggests that because Richard's behaviour is so unpredictable, he should be taught on a one-to-one basis in a different room. Richard however, found the experience of the previous week so traumatic that he is unable to enter the building.

4. Inaccessible buildings and transport

When people think of physical access to buildings, they usually think of lifts and ramps. Recently, architects and buildings managers have become more informed and they are more aware of accessibility issues for blind and deaf people. Accessibility issues for autistic people however, are still relatively unknown. When people are aware of what the issues are, they tend to think that nothing can be done about them. The result is that autistic people's sensory systems are bombarded and over-stimulated on a daily basis, by buildings which take no account of the autistic person's sensory sensitivities. For many autistic people, this exposure results in extreme anxiety. For some it results in total shut down of some of the body's systems, to enable them to cope. The result is viewed by neuro-typical people as 'challenging behaviour' which cannot and should not be tolerated in the neuro-typical world.

Example 3 demonstrates what was viewed at the time, from the medical model perspective, as 'challenging behaviour'. On further examination, using a social model approach, it can be seen that the situation was triggered by issues which were integral to the building design and maintenance, some of which could be altered to make it more accessible to Richard, and other autistic people. Without these alterations, or the ability to affect change in himself, Richard continues to be denied access to his English class. Clearly the inaccessibility of the building presents as a barrier which discriminates against him.

It is often assumed that most people live within walking distance or a short bus ride away from an FE college, when this in fact is not usually the case. In large cities, it may involve a bus ride into the centre of the city and another bus ride to the college campus. In rural areas, the journey may be even longer, more complicated and involve travel to another town. For many autistic people, independent travel on public transport is so fraught with difficulty and uncertainty, that it is difficult to achieve by the age of 16. Indeed, some autistic people may never achieve this skill, regardless of their age or level of intelligence. Many autistic children do not live in the catchment area of the schools which they attend. When this is the case, the child may have been assessed and approved by the LEA as needing assisted transport. When this is the case, then there is normally no difficulty in transferring that arrangement to the FE college, up until the autistic person reaches the age of 19. Problems occur however, when students have not been awarded assisted transport at school (which is often the case if they live within walking distance from school), or if parents do the transporting themselves. Problems also occur if the autistic person is over 19 and has not acquired the skills for independent travel. Many able autistic adults who have advanced skills in many other areas find it impossible to access public transport. It is another societal barrier, which discriminates against them and prevents them from accessing FE.

Removing societal barriers

If we recognize that the barriers which prevent full inclusion for disabled people are located within society and not within the disabled person, then we all as members of society have a responsibility to remove those barriers and to challenge the system which has created them. At first this seems such a huge task that it appears insurmountable, but if we look at the barriers individually, practical solutions become more readily apparent.

It is my belief that improved awareness and education holds the key to changing the attitudes and beliefs which are responsible for creating many of the barriers within society which autistic people experience. It is my experience that when staff and peer awareness of autism is raised, then the bullying that autistic people experience is reduced. When staff receive training which addresses their practical skills and equips them with autism-specific skills and tools, then this is reflected in their practice as well as the autistic student's experience and achievements. When procedures are challenged from positions of quality and good practice, they can be changed. When awareness of autism is increased for architects, planners and buildings managers, then they are better able to produce buildings which are more accessible for autistic people. I am not suggesting that one training session in autism awareness will change everything, but it is a starting point. There will always be people who don't want to engage in the process and who will choose to remain outside all attempts to balance equality within society. I am assuming that if you are reading this book, then you are not one of these people. The responsibility then, for challenging a system which has traditionally seen autistic people as 'less than equal' lies therefore with you.

CHAPTER 2

Which Approach? Ideology, Theory and Practice

I stated in the previous chapter that increasing autism awareness is the first step to achieving 'good practice' in teaching autistic people. 'Good practice', cannot however, be achieved purely by increasing autism awareness. In my experience, the quality of autism awareness courses varies, and it has to be said that some are delivered by trainers who have very little experience of working with autistic people, and who present autism in a negative way, focusing only on the difficulties. Most courses approach the subject from the perspective of the medical model and perpetuate the view that the barriers to inclusion or learning lie within the autistic person, who is therefore responsible for removing them. From this perspective, autistic people are still represented as difficult to manage, with a number of 'challenging behaviours'. When practitioners attend this type of course, there tends to be one of two responses:

1. People come away thinking that they are now an 'expert' on autism and all they need to do is to be aware that autistic people are unable to communicate, imagine, interact etc, or

2. People are so overwhelmed by the complexity of the condition that they think that effective intervention is beyond them. They consequently leave it to other people, who they see as the 'experts'.

Neither response is helpful. I am passionately committed to inclusion, but recognize that this is still a very controversial area with proponents both for and against. The advantages and disadvantages of both are well documented. Generally, it is thought that special schools and colleges have a unique advantage over the mainstream, because they have practitioners who have the specialist knowledge and expertise which enable them to work effectively with autistic students. They also have a high staff: pupil ratio and are more able to create the most suitable learning environment for autistic students. I disagree with this and feel that segregating autistic people treats them as second class, limits their opportunities for interaction and also restricts their educational opportunities. I am however, fiercely defendant of the view that specialist skills are needed to work with autistic people, to the point where I am not prepared to compromise. I do not consider however, that special schools and colleges are synonymous with specialist skills. This view is supported by a National Autistic Society Report (Barnard *et al.* 2002), which found that one in three children in special schools have needs related to autism, yet only 25 per cent of schools in the survey considered that their teachers were adequately trained in this area. I also believe that many mainstream teachers and lecturers have skills which, with the right training and support could be utilized in teaching autistic students. I do recognize that there is a negative aspect to my emphasis on the requirement for specialist skills to work with autistic people, and that this can lead to feelings of defeatism and inadequacy in mainstream teachers and lecturers. Whilst I will not compromise my belief that teaching and supporting autistic people is a highly specialized area of work which requires highly specialized and sophisticated skills, I do accept that it is not necessary for everyone who works with autistic people to have the same level of skill. What is necessary is that the autistic person has immediate access to someone who has these specialist skills and that the mainstream practitioner has immediate access to advice and support from autism specialists. From my experience, this constitutes very effective 'on the job' training for mainstream practitioners.

I have been called both 'ideological' and 'idealistic'. I have no problems with either of these two positions preferring to see the positive application of their use. There are negative connotations which are sometimes attached to both these terms, however. The *Penguin English Dictionary* identifies that 'ideological' is sometimes used to signify 'vague theorizing' or 'impractical views', whilst 'idealistic' can be used to indicate 'unrealistic aspirations'. These negative connotations of what I consider positive attributes, can have the damaging effect of undermining thinking and restricting our vision and practice. If we limit our practice to exclude ideas and vision (which is what ideology is) and if we only aim at what we think is achievable or 'realistic' as opposed to 'idealistic', then we limit our effectiveness. 'Good practice' has to aim high and from this perspective, does not equate with 'good enough practice'. Idealism, gives us the opportunity to seek the 'perfect model which one strives to imitate' (*Penguin English Dictionary*). We may never realize our aspirations, but that in itself shouldn't prevent us from having them. If we are serious about challenging the status quo and improving our practice and the service which we give to autistic people, then we should be prepared to be both ideological and idealistic. This will be reflected in the approach that we take. From this perspective, our approach to working with autistic people ought to be ideological in that there should be a body of ideas which underpins it. It should also be idealistic, in that it should strive for perfection, and in doing so build bridges which challenge and break down barriers of discrimination. I am consequently flattered if I am called either of these things.

An approach that works!

When I first set up the Post-16 provision at The Sheffield College, we were often visited by people from other colleges who were interested in setting up something similar. At some point in the day, they would inevitably ask me what approach we used. I used to find this hugely embarrassing and would mutter something about it being eclectic. The reason that I was embarrassed was because I was not clear in my own mind as to what approach we were advocating. At this point, I was not certain of my ideological perspective. The TEACCH programme (explained later) was very popular at the time (as I think it still is) and I felt pressurized to justify why we weren't using it. There were aspects of a number of different approaches which I found worked some of the time with some of the students who we supported, but there was not any one approach which worked all of the time with all of the students. In reality, the term 'eclectic' did not describe what we were doing as it implies that we were 'mixing and matching' with no clear rationale or body of ideas, underpinning our practice and this was not the case. What we were doing was grounded in theories and knowledge of autism, combined with the belief that the individual should be at the centre of our practice. This required a high level of knowledge and assessment of each student and how they were individually impacted by their autism. We were then applying this to all aspects of the curriculum and adjusting our methods to suit the individual. It was only later that I came to recognize this as 'person centred' in approach.

Autistic people tell us how it is impossible to separate the person from the autism:

> Autism isn't something a person has, or a shell that a person is trapped inside. There's no normal child hidden behind the autism. Autism is a way of being. It is pervasive; it colours every experience, every sensation, perception, thought, emotion and encounter, every aspect of existence. It is not possible to separate the autism from the person – and if it were possible, the person you'd have left would not be the same person you started with. (Sinclair 1993)

It seems right therefore that any teaching or support offered to autistic people has to focus on the person. In doing this, it will also embrace the autism. Jordan and Powell (1997, p.19) caution against a 'recipe approach' and describe how the approach can become the focus of the teaching to the exclusion of the autism. They also point out that it is equally misguided to focus on the autism to the exclusion of the teaching. A balance has to be found.

It seems appropriate at this point to emphasize the dangers of ignorance and arrogance. To work with autistic people and know nothing about autism can be damaging, but working with autistic people and thinking that we are the 'expert' can be equally, if not more damaging. It is essential to underpin our practice with knowledge gained, from academic and theoretical sources, but this type of knowledge has to be tried and tested against knowledge gained from the practical 'live it' experiences of autistic people. We are not, and never will be 'experts' in this field. However much we know, autistic people will always teach us more.

Invariably, after delivering a training session, people will ask me which books on the suggested reading list accompanying the session, would I recommend as essential reading. My answer is always the same – 'the autobiographies' of such people as Donna Williams, Temple Grandin, Luke Jackson and Liane Holliday Willey. These accounts give us knowledge and insight into the world of autism, which we as neuro-typical people can only glimpse at. It is an essential glimpse however, which I consider should inform all our practice. After that, the theories can be critically examined and applied to our understanding and practical application.

It is not my intention to undermine the importance of the role of theoretical or academic knowledge in the pursuit of good practice. In fact, I consider it essential that all autism awareness courses should, in addition to including the personal accounts already mentioned, include academic study of the following theories:

- Wing's Triad of Impairments.

- Theory of Mind.

- Central Coherence Theory.

(These are examined in more detail in Chapter 5: Staff Training.)

In many ways, the idea of different approaches for autism comes out of the medical model (see Chapter 1). This model seeks to diagnose, find out the cause and cure the condition. When it is unable to cure, then it seeks to manage the condition by approaching it in a certain way. The way that the 'management' of a person's autism is approached depends on a number of factors such as personal, political and ideological beliefs, as well as organizational and financial constraints. When a child is diagnosed as being autistic, the reality is that there is very little choice for most parents. Choice is restricted by the information and advice which parents have, and the resources, both practical and financial which are available. Most parents have little knowledge of autism at the time of diagnosis. Some have the qualities which enable them to research, question and put their viewpoint forward, and some are able to negotiate the financial resources to provide an approach which fits their researched criteria. The reality for most parents however, is that their choice is severely restricted, not only by financial constraints, but also by the confusing minefield of different competing information and approaches which they have to negotiate. If they are clear about an approach, then they have to battle for the limited resources which are available to them. In terms of education, unless they are prepared to 'home educate', which some parents feel is the only choice open to them, then they have to accept what is offered by the Local Education Authority in the first instance, and as the child becomes older, the FE college or university.

It is my view that there is one factor which is fundamental to any approach to working with autistic people and that is that understanding the person should form the basis of the approach. With that in mind, it seems an appropriate point to explain briefly some of the more popular approaches to working with autistic people. The two main approaches which currently seem to dominate professional practice in the area of autism are: TEACCH and ABA (Applied Behavioural Analysis), now associated with the Lovaas approach. Both stem from the viewpoint that autism is a life-long condition, and both take a medical model approach to addressing behaviour. The third approach I will look at in this chapter is Options. Like the previous two, the Options approach comes from within the medical model, but unlike them, it takes the view that autism can be cured, and addresses itself to this.

Division TEACCH

TEACCH stands for:

> **T** – Treatment
>
> **E** – and Education of
>
> **A** – Autistic and related
>
> **C** – Communication handicapped
>
> **CH** – CHildren.

Division TEACCH started in 1966 as a project within the Department of Psychiatry of the School of Medicine at the University of North Carolina. By 1972, it had become the first comprehensive state-wide community-based programme of services for children and adults with autism and other similar developmental disorders. Since then, TEACCH has developed into a 'cradle to the grave' service, which offers a broad range of services to autistic people and their families. This includes amongst other things, diagnosis and assessment, individualized 'treatment' programmes, social skills training, vocational training, parent training and counselling. In addition, TEACCH has developed an ongoing active research programme and multidisciplinary training for professionals working with autistic people and their families.

The primary aim of the TEACCH programme is to help to prepare autistic people to live or work more effectively. Special emphasis is given to helping people with autism and their families live together more effectively by reducing or removing 'autistic behaviours'. Structured teaching is seen as an important priority, because it is thought to suit the 'culture of autism' more effectively than any other technique.

The principles and concepts guiding the TEACCH system have been summarized as:

- *Improved adaptation*: through the two strategies of improving skills by means of education and of modifying the environment to accommodate deficits.

- *Parent collaboration*: parents work with professionals as co-therapists for their children so that techniques can be continued at home.

- *Assessment for individualized treatment*: unique educational programmes are designed for all individuals on the basis of regular assessments of abilities.

- *Structured teaching*: it has been found that children with autism benefit more from a structured educational environment than from free approaches.

- *Skill enhancement*: assessment identifies emerging skills and work then focuses upon these. This approach is also applied to staff and parent training.

- *Cognitive and behaviour therapy*: educational procedures are guided by theories of cognition and behaviour suggesting that difficult behaviour may result from underlying problems in perception and understanding.

- *Generalist training*: professionals in the TEACCH system are trained as generalists who understand the whole child, and do not specialize as psychologists, speech therapists etc.

(National Autistic Society 1993, revised in 2003)

Success is a very subjective term and is difficult to measure, but by most terms, TEACCH is viewed as being successful. It currently implements 'exemplary services' for over 5000 autistic people and their families in North Carolina (www.teacch.com, accessed 02/12/04). It is also an international centre for interdisciplinary training in autism, offering training programmes on diagnosis and assessment, structured teaching, educational services, residential and vocational programmes as well as parent training (ibid).

TEACCH became very popular in the UK in the late 1980s and early 1990s and several schools, including the National Autistic Society Schools have provided staff training and incorporated elements of the programme, particularly the structured teaching element, into their classrooms. There is however, no similar life-long service in the UK. This, I think forms the basis for most of the criticisms and concerns regarding the approach. The high level of structure provided by TEACCH offers a practical strategy which is useful and can be effectively applied in most settings. The problem seems to have occurred because teachers, sometimes with only a little knowledge of autism, have taken to the approach wholeheartedly, seeing it as offering an immediate 'fix' to classroom problems. In this way, the approach, rather than the education of the autistic child has become the focus. In at least one instance, in their enthusiasm for the approach, TEACCH has become a subject timetabled as part of the curriculum, rather than the means to accessing the curriculum and developing the full potential of the autistic person. There is also a significant problem in that the structure offered by TEACCH effectively acts as a prop for the autistic person, without addressing cognitive processes. Without the support of the wider programme, there is a danger that when the structure is removed, the autistic person is left with no prop. This results in the wider criticism that the TEACCH programme is not one of education, but one of training, as it gives no responsibility, choice or control to the autistic person. It also leads to the criticism that whilst TEACCH may be a suitable approach for less able, severely autistic people, it is not suitable for more able individuals.

With regard to FE, it is rarely possible and probably not desirable in terms of teaching independence skills, to structure the environment in the way or to the level which following the TEACCH approach requires. It is rarely used in FE settings, as a result. That is not to say that there are no lessons to be learnt from TEACCH. In particular, it takes the autistic person as its starting point, focusing on their individual skills, interests, strengths and needs. It recognizes the need to understand autism and in many instances provides successful intervention strategies, which enable the further development of skills. These are valuable aspects of the approach which can be more flexibly applied to the FE setting.

ABA (Applied Behaviour Analysis)

Applied Behaviour Analysis (ABA) grew out of the 'behavioural school' of psychology and in the field of autism is usually considered to be synonymous with the Lovaas approach. Lovaas began his work in the 1970s, but his work developed from the work of B.F. Skinner, whose main body of work took place in the middle decades of the 20th century. We can in turn, trace the origins of Skinner's work, back to the familiar 'Pavlov's dogs' experiments, and the notion of 'conditioning', which took place in the last decades of the 19th century. Skinner was a biologist who applied strict scientific principles to studying learning and behaviour. He put forward the view that all behaviour could be explained as resulting from what he termed ABC: *Antecedents*, which are the conditions which exist which make it appropriate for something to happen. *Behaviour* is the action which can be observed, and *Consequences* are the things that come about as a result of the behaviour. Central to this approach, is the role of 'reinforcement', which can be positive or negative. Both types of reinforcement are covered by the term 'consequences'. Skinner suggested that teachers or parents, who actively work to organize the learning environments of their students by following the ABC approach, and reinforcing appropriate responses, can accelerate their students' learning. This has been very influential in the field of education and as a result, most teachers will have studied this theory at some time during their training. It was particularly popular during the 1960s and 1970s, which is when Lovaas began applying it to young autistic children. It is thought to be particularly useful for intervention in the early years, and some local authorities and specialist schools still apply it rigorously as their main tool of 'early intervention'.

To be most effective, the programme should be extremely intensive, and incorporate many planned opportunities for learning skills throughout the day. These opportunities should be planned precisely and delivered by highly skilled parents and professionals. Proponents of the approach recognize that for many children, the optimum benefit may involve 30 to 40 hours per week of direct one-to-one skilled teaching. Ideally, if the approach is implemented before the age of three, the programme should last for two to three years, but might need to be longer, if the child is older at the commencement of its implementation. There is a strong emphasis on language, communication and social skills, throughout the programme.

It is essential to the child's success, that there is consistency amongst practitioners and that everyone involved with the child works together as a team, so that the child is engaged in the approach at all times.

In terms of practical skills and classroom management, the process of arranging antecedents and consequences (that is managing the learning environment and providing reinforcement) is the basic unit of all successful teaching for all skills, for autistic children. Food, praise and hugs, are commonly used as reinforcers with the development and addition of more sophisticated items such as tokens, or credits. There is a proviso that all teaching should end successfully, so goals set should be attainable.

On a personal level, I do not respond well to ABA (no pun intended). I mentioned 'Pavlov's dogs' intentionally at the beginning of this chapter, because I have met many parents who are greatly offended by this approach and who express the view that whilst it may work very well for dogs, it is insulting and offensive to apply it to the education of children. On a professional level, I echo this view. As an approach, I consider that it fulfils the criteria for 'training', not teaching and I see very little place for it in educational programmes. In terms of FE, the high level of intensity required by the approach, together with the emphasis on early and prolonged participation, cannot really be accommodated in the FE setting and it does little to develop cognitive processing, nor lend itself well to the fostering of independence skills. In practice, it is recognized that the change in behaviour has a limited life, and that without the continued use of reinforcers, becomes 'extinct'. My feelings therefore are that in terms of an educational approach, it is very limited. I do however, consider that there is a role for behaviourist approaches in the immediate but temporary, management of harmful behaviours. Such intervention should always be accompanied by a more holistic approach, which views the behaviour as a form of communication, and addresses itself to the whole person, not only to the elimination of the unwanted behaviour. In my experience, most 'unreasonable' and consequently unwanted behaviours, when viewed from an autistic perspective become perfectly logical and reasonable. If we search for explanations from outside of the autistic person then solutions become easier to find.

Options (Son-Rise Program)

Unlike the other two approaches discussed above, the Options or Son-Rise approach, takes the view that autism can be cured. It developed in America, as a parental response or challenge to the prognosis which was given to an autistic child, Raun Kaufman, who is now a 'cured' adult with a 'genius IQ'. Options is now referred to as a treatment programme and is called The Autism Treatment Programme of America. The programme advocates a system of treatment and education which is non-confrontational, home-based and extremely intense. Parents describe a daily therapy programme in which they are supported by other Son-Rise trained carers, usually volunteers, for ideally eight hours a day. It claims to be child-centred, and accepting of the autistic child, where they are at, and on their terms, whilst at the same time setting desired goals and outcomes. It addresses behaviour by distinguishing between behaviour which needs to be changed as opposed to that which parents want to change. The essence of the approach is that parents need to understand their child completely, by getting into their world. From here, they are able to gain the child's trust and then the child will join them in their world. This is achieved by removing the child from 'the world' and providing therapy through the form of play, which takes place in a room which is made to specific Son-Rise guidelines. This is essentially one of low arousal, with bare walls and linoleum covered floor, toys on shelves which are out of reach to the child, and mirrors on the walls. It is claimed that this low arousal environment aids concentration and the ability to interact socially. The principles underlying the programme, as de-scribed in the Son-Rise website are:

1. Joining in a child's repetitive and ritualistic behaviours supplies the key to unlocking the mystery of these behaviours and facilitates eye contact, social development and the inclusion of others in play.

2. Utilizing a child's own motivation advances learning and builds the foundation for education and skills acquisition.

3. Teaching through interactive play results in effective and meaningful socialization and communication.

4. Using energy, excitement and enthusiasm engages the child and inspires a continuous love of learning and interaction.

5. Employing a non-judgemental and optimistic attitude maximizes the child's enjoyment, attention and desire throughout their Son-Rise Program.

6.   Placing the parent as the child's most important and lasting resource provides a consistent and compelling focus for training, education and inspiration.

7.   Creating a safe, distraction-free work/play area facilitates the optimal environment for learning and growth.

There seems to be some contradictions in this approach. It claims to give control to the child and to be child-centred, yet it restricts choice, by putting toys out of reach and limiting all activities to the 'therapy room'. It claims to accept the child for what she or he is, yet it focuses on the need to change the child. The distinction between the need and the want to change seems somehow vague and unsatisfactory. There are many criticisms but the purpose of this chapter is to examine how the approach can be applied to FE. (A detailed critical analysis can be found on http://www.rsaffran.tripod.com/sonrise.html.)

Like the other two approaches discussed, the Son-Rise programme is not a short-term fix, is best suited to early intervention and is extremely intensive. Initially, this suggests that it does not lend itself well to FE. It is also couched in language which does not fit the FE culture and ethos, or the notion of adult learners. However, there are many positives to this approach, and it is my experience that in practice, if we can look beyond the things which sit uncomfortably with us, there are others aspects which we can adapt and apply.

In the beginning of this chapter, I described what I considered to be the ideal approach for working with autistic students as follows:

• to be grounded in knowledge of autism and personal accounts

• to be person-centred.

I also clarified that this required:

• effective forms of autism-specific assessments, curricula and teaching methods.

These I consider to be essential factors to an 'approach that works'. If understanding the person and placing them at the centre of all intervention strategies becomes the focus, then the approach becomes secondary to the overall needs of the autistic person. This will then avoid the problems which are inherent in an eclectic approach, and ensure that everything that is done fits together as a coherent whole. In this way, everything, from the curriculum to the type of support, contributes to the overall aims for the autistic person.

What does it mean to be person-centred?

Person-centred means that the autistic person is not slotted into a ready-made provision, where they may be a 'square peg in a round hole'. Instead, they become the focus of all planning for a provision which is developed around them. In this way, their choices and preferences are taken into account and honoured. 'Person-centred' is entirely compatible with inclusion, which is not synonymous with integration, but is in itself a person-centred concept where providers match their provision to the needs of the individual learner. By this definition, all institutions which define themselves as 'inclusive' should be person-centred. Traditionally, autistic people have been effectively excluded from this process, because they have been seen as being 'unable to make choices' or 'unable to communicate' or 'unaware of their needs' when in fact the underlying problem is the difficulty which neuro-typical people have in communicating with them. As a result, choices have been made on their behalf, by parents or professionals who have their best interests at heart. Inevitably, this has led to a 'we know best' approach, which doesn't always fit with what the autistic person wants. The frustration which the autistic person experiences as a result is then often expressed through behaviour which is labelled as 'challenging'. This then initiates further discussion, planning and decision making, which does not include the autistic person's views, which in turn leads to more 'challenging' behaviour. The end result of this cycle is often that the autistic person cannot be accommodated in mainstream and is excluded. This is then easily justified by the high level of discussion, planning and support which has taken place and the need to protect the autistic person and others from inappropriate behaviour. In this way, well-intentioned, caring professional people miss the point. Support is only supportive if it is the support which the autistic person needs and wants. An autistic man recently described his frustrations to me about exactly this as 'it is like going into the chemist with a headache and coming out with a plaster'. This situation often arises in FE, because we claim to be inclusive, without being person-centred. We then operate in a 'one size fits all' system, which like the chemist offers a plaster, because we do not have pain killers.

Being person-centred

The key to being person-centred is 'knowing the person'. This presents challenges for professionals when working with autistic people, as autism by its very nature affects every thing which we use to form social relationships. It is often assumed that because an autistic person is at college, then they have Asperger syndrome as opposed to autism and that as a result their needs are less, and they need less skilled support. This is inaccurate and misguided on both counts. It is my experience that the whole autism spectrum is represented at college, and that autistic students, wherever their diagnosis places them on the autism spectrum, all need highly skilled, individually planned support. The key to knowing the autistic person is being able to communicate effectively with them. It is true that people who have a diagnosis of 'high-functioning autism' or Asperger syndrome are able to articulate language, but that is often taken as an indicator that they have little impairment of communication. As long ago as 1968, David Abercrombie wrote the now famous quotation 'We speak with our vocal organs but we converse with our entire bodies. Conversation consists of much more than a simple interchange of spoken words' (Abercrombie 1968, p.55). In fact, we now know that less than 10 per cent of communication is verbal. Despite knowing this however, we continue to make assumptions about people, based purely on their verbal communication. We continue, amongst other things, to assess people's intelligence and social status, based on how they talk. We also rely heavily on the written and spoken word, particularly in education. This is where the Options approach has a lot to offer us in FE. Effective communication with an autistic person involves getting alongside them and entering their world, whatever label has been attached to them. I am not suggesting that we shut ourselves up in a cell-type room with the autistic person and mirror all their behaviours, but I am suggesting that neuro-typical people need to take the initiative if we are to improve our communication with autistic people. We need to break out of the confines of a verbal culture and be creative in our approach to communication. We also need to be able to work in partnership with others who know the autistic person well. This again, goes against the ethos of FE, where parental involvement, especially if the student is over 18, is not so readily sought.

The following is an example of one of the most enjoyable communication experiences which I have had, with a very articulate, very academically able 11-year-old autistic boy. I include it here, because even though it is strictly speaking still verbal, the words themselves had very little to do with what was being communicated. It also will always stick in my mind for the pure pleasure that we both received from it. I am convinced that it also provided a breakthrough in my relationship with this boy. It enabled us to develop a very close, effective working relationship, which was based on trust and understanding, where he was able to communicate his needs and wants very clearly. We are still in touch, eight years later.

Boy: Woof.

Me: Woof, woof.

Boy: (Smiling now) Woof, woof ,woof.

Me: (Also smiling) Woof, woof, woof, woof.

Boy: (looking at me and smiling) Woof, woof, woof, woof woof.

Me: (Trying to keep count but still smiling) Woof, woof, woof, woof woof, woof.

Boy: (looking at me and really smiling) Woof, woof, woof, woof woof, woof, woof.

Me: (Because I had totally lost count at this point) Miaaaow!

Both of us fell apart laughing.

Communication skills

Good communication skills don't just happen (although some people do seem to be naturally better communicators than others), they can also be learnt. From the person-centred perspective, they should be learnt from the autistic person. In my experience, one of the best ways to do this is through a system of 'profiling'. Some practitioners view communication as a self-contained entity which can be profiled separately from other aspects of the person. I take the view that the way we communicate is an expression of who we are. It conveys information about the way that we feel, think and perceive ourselves and the world, as well as where we come from and who we are. From this perspective, a more holistic type of profiling is necessary. It is important to mention here that profiling is not an end in itself. It is rather a means to an end. Profiling is a tool, which at its best, provides a way to understanding and communicating with the autistic person. It is not in itself being person-centred. If used correctly, it can form one of the foundation stones of a person-centred approach. Once completed, it should be dynamic and should be used to inform all practice.

Profiling

I do not wish to be prescriptive here as there are a number of ways which profiling can be achieved. Some people prefer a formal, structured approach which lends itself to using a standardized system; others prefer a more relaxed process, based on observation, discussion and reflection. Whatever personal preference is taken, an effective profile ought to involve the autistic person and those who know them well, and it also ought to consider the following points about the autistic person:

- previous experience and response to it

- wants and desires

- ability and potential

- thinking style

- use and understanding of language

- use and understanding of all areas of non-verbal communication

- sensory processing and perceptions

- social skills

- specific talents, skills or fascinations

- anxiety levels and potential triggers

- behaviour as a form of communication.

It is appropriate here to emphasize that profiling is not something that anyone can do. I have seen situations where practitioners who are skilled at working with learning disabled students have failed miserably at the task, because they have not recognized the fundamental differences in autistic people. Profiling must be informed by autism-specific knowledge and skills. Without these, the information gained can be superficial, relatively worthless and potentially harmful. It is my view that profiling should not be undertaken lightly and then, only by an autism specialist.

The process of profiling

Information gathering

Ideally, information should be gathered from as many sources as possible, prior to the student coming to college. Someone from the college should have been involved at the student's transition review, which takes place in Year 9 of school, and at subsequent annual reviews (if the student has a Statement of Educational Needs). These would have included parents, careers advisors, teachers and support staff, and sometimes educational psychologists and speech and language therapists, and increasingly, the young autistic person themselves. In some instances, there is no prior involvement, but transition passports or individual transition programmes are used for this purpose. In other instances, for a number of reasons, there is no information accompanying an autistic person to college. In such circumstances, the profiling has to start from scratch and would involve gleaning as much information from as many people mentioned above as is reasonably possible. It is important to emphasize here that the purpose of this is not to develop a preconceived idea of the autistic person, or to look for problems. It must always be kept in mind that the purpose of this information gathering is to get to know the autistic person so that the best assessment of their needs can be made. It is also important to emphasize that this should not be about making judgements.

I described profiling earlier in this chapter (see p.55) as a tool, which provides a way of getting to know an autistic person. I also described it as a dynamic process rather than a 'one-off' task. It is a process which should be continually updated to keep it in line with the development and progression of the autistic person. I have seen many instances in FE, when information has been gathered about a student and an excellent profile has been drawn up at the beginning of the academic year. This profile, though very relevant at the time, is then the profile which informs all practice throughout the student's time at college. I have also seen profiles which have not engaged or involved the autistic person at any point in the development process. This type of profiling is not part of a person-centred approach. It is however, entirely acceptable to draw up a temporary profile at the beginning of the student's first year in FE, which is based on the information gathered prior to admission. This temporary profile can be used to inform and guide the gathering of further information, and influence practice.

Once enrolled at college, it is important that the information gathering should continue, in order to ensure that the information which is already given is relevant to the new situation. This continued information gathering will now come directly from the autistic person themselves. It can be gathered through the following ways:

- listening to the autistic person

- observing the autistic person

- searching for meaning in their behaviour

- asking questions using a variety of different media

- discussing with the autistic person (using a variety of forms of communication).

Assessing the information

If the information gathered is to be valid and useful, it will have to be analysed and assessed and then put into a format which has a practical use. If this is not structured, controlled and informed by knowledge of autism, then there is a real danger of it being nothing more than 'opinions'. I would not wish to devalue other people's opinions, but again stress the significance of this process in the life of the autistic person. The purpose of gathering information is to enable a better knowledge of that person in terms of what their wants and needs are. The purpose of assessing the information gathered is to enable the autistic person to achieve their goals and their potential. To do this requires more than just 'opinions,' it requires a framework which is based in a sound knowledge of autism.

The following is an example of the type of questions which should form part of that framework:

1. What does the person want to achieve in life?

2. What support/coping strategies has the person found effective in the past?

3. Does the person use verbal communication to communicate with others? If so, how effectively? It is helpful at this point to identify and discuss areas of misuse, misinterpretation or misunderstanding.

4. It is the person aware of the role of non-verbal cues in communication? If so, are they able to use and interpret them effectively? Again, possible areas of misuse, misinterpretation or misunderstanding should be identified and discussed.

5. Does the person experience any hyper- or hypo-sensitivity in any of the five sensory areas? If so identify what and where and when?

6. What environmental triggers provoke anxiety? These should be identified and listed.

7. What strategies work in reducing anxiety? Again, these should be identified and documented.

8. Is behaviour an indicator of emotional and/or sensory sensitivity? If so, identify.

9. What is repeated behaviour communicating? Identify and document.

10. Does the person have any specific talents, skills or fascinations? If so, what?

11. What is the person's thinking style? For example: logical; visual; literal; inventive; creative etc.

12. At what academic stage is the person at?

Many similar assessment tools suggest some sort of grading system at this point. The purpose of this is to measure the autistic person's level of impairment in different areas. Typically, these may be numerical scores, or phrases like 'working towards' or 'not yet acquired'. These scores then give a level which records progress and improvement in those areas. The format suggested above does not do this because it encourages the autistic person's involvement in setting the level of desired attainment, rather than working towards set social norms.

If the profiling process were to end here, it would just be a time-consuming paper exercise, with possibly negative implications for the autistic person. To be part of a person-centred approach to working with autistic people, profiling must inform practice. The next stage in the process is therefore making recommendations.

Making recommendations

Chapter 1 identified that the barriers which disable autistic people are not located in the people themselves, but are to be found in a society which discriminates against them. If this is the case, then the solutions or the recommendations which will remove those barriers will also be found within society. Recommendations should not therefore focus on the need for the autistic person to change, for example 'to work on their ability to learn how to use euphemisms and metaphors'. Rather, they should focus on what needs to be put in place to enable the autistic person to understand language (including euphemisms and metaphors) better. Recommendations should therefore do the following:

1. Identify strategies that are known to work for the person.

2. Suggest the type of support which needs to be put in place.

3. Make suggestions for more effective ways of communicating with the person.

4. Identify ways of motivating the person.

5. Identify triggers for anxiety and suggest ways of minimizing them.

6. Suggest ways of adapting teaching to suit thinking and learning style.

7. Suggest ways of altering or adapting the environment to take account of sensory issues.

8. Suggest ways of avoiding emotional hypersensitivity.

9. Suggest ways of interpreting and understanding behaviour.

10. Provide aims which are targeted at maximising and achieving potential.

Making recommendations is of no use if there is not a process of evaluation and reassessment in place. This in turn will result in updating the profile, in order to accommodate and record change. A true person-centred approach cannot recommend how often a profile will need to be updated. In theory, it will depend entirely on the given situation with each individual student. Having said that, I have found that in practice, updating profiles tends to fall into three categories as follows:

- Those that are updated annually.

- Those that are updated termly.

- Those that are updated half-termly.

Often, when barriers are removed and autism-specific support is put in place, there is a dramatic difference in the autistic student's ability to engage with their learning environment. This results in the need for early re-evaluation and reassessment. This may settle down to a more gradual progression. However, it is my experience that autistic people's learning style is particularly suited to sudden rapid leaps in terms of progress and achievement. When this is the case, it must guide the timing for evaluation and reassessment. I have on one occasion had to update a student's profile after only three weeks.

Evaluation and reassessment

Grading systems can improve the efficiency of the process of evaluation, but in my view are process driven rather than person-centred. The process which I have outlined is cyclical, where the evaluation would replicate the information gathering part of the process. In this way the process is continuous and dynamic. Practitioners are continually engaged in observing, discussing and reflecting on both their practice and the autistic student's response to it. The process is also very creative, as it involves continuously thinking of strategies which remove barriers and enable the autistic student to have full inclusion.

Summary

There is no single approach that works all of the time for all autistic people, but there is a danger that a 'pick and mix' approach will lead to conflict and confusion, both for the autistic person and those working with them. Any approach to working with autistic people must understand and respect the person with autism and place them at the centre of the approach. It must also understand the nature of autism and how it impacts on the individual. It should focus on removing the barriers which cause anxiety, stress and 'challenging behaviour'. The overall aim of any approach should be to enable the autistic person to succeed in line with their wants, needs and potential. From this point of view, I think that it is OK to be both ideological and idealistic.

CHAPTER 3

Developing an Inclusive Specialist Team

There is a misconception that inclusive is synonymous with integration and that specialist is synonymous with segregation. Neither is true. There is however, still confusion as to what the term 'inclusive' really does mean and an internet search will reveal that there are many varied definitions which add to the confusion.

In Hesmondhalgh and Breakey (2001, p.191) I defined inclusion as 'a practical issue as well as an ideological one' and I wrote that:

> Inclusion within an educational setting, means finding the best match, or fit between the individual student's learning requirement and the educational provision. Unlike integration, which means fitting the student into the provision, inclusion means devising or redesigning the learning environment to match the individual student's learning requirement.

I stand by that definition, which was not of my own thinking, but was guided by my understanding of the Tomlinson Report 1996 gained from the Centre for Studies on Inclusive Education (CSIE). The phrase I would like to focus on in this chapter is: 'devising or redesigning the learning environment to match the individual student's learning requirement'.

I am very conscious that in the previous chapter I have emphasized the need for practitioners working with autistic people to have specialist knowledge and skills. I am also conscious that in doing this

I might have frightened some readers into thinking that this is a job which is so highly specialized that it is beyond them. I apologize if that is the case and would encourage you not to give up at this point. I do believe that this is a specialized area of work, but if you are reading this book, then you are one of the people who have already recognized that you have a need for greater knowledge and skills in this area. You have also identified yourself as someone who has the potential for becoming a 'specialist' in this field. Working with autistic students, particularly within mainstream is one of the most difficult and challenging tasks that anyone can have. It is also one of the most fascinating and rewarding. One of the reasons for this is that there is always more to learn. If you listen to and learn from the autistic students you work with, you will find that each person teaches you something new, which you can add to your repertoire of skills. Becoming an autism specialist does not happen overnight. It takes years of practice, but you will get there!

I am convinced that supporting autistic people in FE colleges requires specialist skills, and this view has been confirmed by my experience since leaving FE. I am now approached by many colleges, who recognize that they do not have the skills to support their autistic students. Time and time again, they are recognizing the need for ongoing specialist training which will lead to the development of specialist teams, which will more effectively meet the needs of this particular group of students.

I described the setting up and the first year of the autism specialist support team at The Sheffield College, in *Access and Inclusion for Children with Autistic Spectrum Disorders* (Hesmondhalgh and Breakey 2001). I knew at the time that I was extremely privileged to be able to set it up from scratch with only two students, and anticipated that it would grow fairly quickly. No one could have anticipated that it would have grown to support 46 students, with a team of 15 staff across five college sites, in as little as four years. There were a number of different reasons for this rapid increase, one of which was the rise in the numbers of students who had a diagnosis of Asperger syndrome. This is not peculiar to Sheffield; growth of autistic students will be echoed in all other FE colleges. Because of this, at most colleges, numbers of autistic students will already be quite significant, and the 'starting small' model which was described at Sheffield is probably no longer a viable proposition. This chapter will therefore provide guidelines for developing an autism specialist service from within an already existing generic support model.

As I travel around the country to different FE colleges, I have discovered that they have many different approaches to supporting disabled students. There is of course a requirement that any autism specialist provision has to fit in with the existing organizational structure. Current legislation also quite rightly requires that all service provision does not treat any disabled person unfavourably compared with a non-disabled person, and that reasonable adjustments be put in place which ensures that this does not happen. This is a great strength for the development of any autism specialist provision, as all organizations have a vested interest in complying with the law. Support constitutes a 'reasonable adjustment' and in the case of the autistic person, the specialist nature of this support needs to be recognized for the reasons already given in the previous chapter. Many colleges are now recognizing that the 'one size fits all' type of support does not constitute an effective reasonable adjustment, so it is consequently an opportune time to encourage the growth of autism specialists.

It is my experience that potential autism specialists emerge within existing FE support services, almost by a process of 'natural selection'. These are the people who have first of all developed an interest in autistic people, which has led to the desire to increase their knowledge in the subject area, which has in turn led to the development of practical skills. Whatever different organizational structures are in place in different colleges, this is really of no consequence as it is the provision of a skilled specialist support service which is essential. From this perspective, it really doesn't matter who provides the support. They could be called lecturers, learner support assistants, instructors, or anything else, but the nature and quality of the support provided is essential if the autistic person is to access FE and achieve in line with his or her potential. I would like to clarify here that I do not mean that the people who provide the support are not important, or that as is often wrongly assumed, that anyone can perform this role. On the contrary, supporting autistic students, or any disabled students for that matter is a highly skilled job, which requires a high level of intelligence and skill. In terms of FE, the value of additional support staff is rarely recognized or given the status which it deserves. As a result, most 'hands on' support is separated from the more academic roles and is awarded in some instances the status of 'care'. At best, the bulk of additional support which disabled students receive within FE colleges comes from care assistants, or learning/learner support assistants. These people are usually employed on inferior contracts to teaching staff, on a 'term time only' basis, often receiving half the salary of a basic full-time contracted lecturer. In addition, there is no obvious career progression route. This inevitably has an impact on staff recruitment and retention.

Setting up an autism specialist service

In most instances, autism specialist teams, if colleges have them, tend to have evolved from the existing provision. Few have the luxury of starting from scratch. As a result, they bring with them 'baggage' from the main provision which is often unhelpful. There is still the misguided view that additional support is an 'easy option' because it requires less preparation and evaluation time than more academic teaching. Clearly the people who voice this view do not have an informed understanding of additional support. Both roles involve preparation and evaluation, and require hard work and dedication as well as a high level of knowledge and practical skill. If you work in a college which recognizes this, you are extremely fortunate. It is my experience however, that this is not a view which is shared by the majority of FE lecturers and managers. Because of this, most support teams, whether generic or specialist, begin from the misinformed, but disadvantaged starting point of low status. This is unfortunately a position which first of all has to be rectified, if additional support teams are to provide a service of excellence for disabled students.

Autism challenges us to rethink radically everything we do professionally. Because of this, if we are to achieve any level of excellence and good practice in the service we provide, we will have to challenge any structures within the institutions in which we work which limit, restrict and discriminate against autistic students. For most of us, challenging authority, especially when coming from a position of sub-ordinance, is not comfortable. It is also time consuming, exhausting and detracts us from our work. However, if we are to break down the barriers which disable our students and limit their access to achieving their potential, challenge we must! Before we can do this however, we need to regain our position of equality within the institution in which we work, so that we can challenge from a position of authority. This involves removing the baggage which has first of all placed us in the position of unequal status and subordination. In other words, it requires us to regain our professional status. My experience at The Sheffield College suggests that if it is to be truly successful, this must be done on two fronts. The first is with our mainstream colleagues. The second is with senior management, at the highest level.

The first is relatively easy to achieve, but the second is more diffi-cult as it involves 'playing the political game'. Experience has taught me that the delivery of a 'service of excellence', which is what autistic students deserve, depends on more than the knowledge, skills and hard work of the people who deliver it. The provision of good prac-tice is also subject to the whims and decisions of the people who are in power, be they in national government, or within the organization. As a result, education and disability cannot be apolitical. If we are serious about inclusion for autistic people, then we have a responsi-bility to challenge the barriers which exist for them, at all levels. This includes the highest levels within society. This may seem daunting, and it is political, but it does not mean that we must all become mili-tant and antagonistic. On the contrary; it is much more effective to demonstrate to senior management, that the specialist service which we provide serves the needs and interests of the organization as a whole. To do this involves increasing their awareness of autism and the needs of autistic students. Most senior managers have little aware-ness of the nature of support so there is a need to educate them in this area also.

Regaining professional status and recognition

Senior management

The autism service at The Sheffield College was initiated by senior managers who were not autism specialists, but who anticipated a growing need and had a vision for a specialist service. When a programme of 'downsizing' led to their retirement, and the appointment of new managers who did not share this awareness and vision, I was too involved in the practical issues of my role and my own vision, to recognize my responsibility in this wider area.

In Chapter 1, I described the bureaucracy which exists in FE, which effectively acts as a barrier to good communication. This bureaucracy, together with the protective mechanisms of a hierarchical structure, often makes it difficult for front-line workers such as lecturers and learner support assistants to communicate directly with senior managers, however approachable they may be on a personal level. This creates the situation where individuals tend to communicate with their line managers, who in turn communicate with the next tier of management, who communicate with the next tier and so on. This is not an effective way of achieving the objectives of increasing the awareness of senior managers and demonstrating to them that the specialist service which we provide is in the interests of the organization as a whole and I would caution against it. The potential for misunderstanding and miscommunication which this type of communication network produces is demonstrated simply in Figure 1.2 in Chapter 1. This figure illustrates how the message can be altered and diluted in the process of dissemination. It does not however, explain the effects of intention, motivation and manipulation of the sender and receiver of the message. At each level of the decoding and encoding process, the message is subject to change, according to how it is received and subsequently sent by each individual in the chain. Individuals bring with them their own agendas, interpretations and desired outcomes. These inevitably affect the meaning of the message at every level of dissemination throughout the management hierarchy. It is inevitable that one of the factors involved in putting other people's points of view forward, is the implication or the cost that this will have for oneself. I prefer to take people at face value and to take them at their word, but my experience is that only very rarely is someone sufficiently altruistic to support another person or group of people, if it is not part of their personal agenda, or incurs a personal cost. Because of this, I would suggest that if you have lower management responsibility for supporting autistic students, then you do not get drawn into this hierarchical communication network. Your passion and vision will inevitably become distorted by the messenger's own agenda, and the message which senior managers eventually receive will be of a much poorer and diluted quality. In addition, no one who is not an autism specialist will understand the needs of the service which you provide as well as you do, and you could feel let down by their representation. Because of this, I would advise that you take personal responsibility for ensuring that the people at the top tiers of the organization are kept fully informed of:

1.   who your team is

2.   what your team does

3.   why and how you do it, and

4.   what your team achieves.

This does not have to be conveyed in a confrontational way or make you unpopular, but can be presented as a celebration of your team's successes.

There is a problem for us here, which we must overcome and which can be aided by our understanding of theories on autism. Additional support traditionally attracts more females than males, whilst senior managers are predominantly male. We have long since recognized that this situation has come about through gender inequalities within society, rather than gender ability. We have also moved from viewing gender equality as being synonymous with gender similarity. Most of us now recognize that men and women are different in many ways other than the obvious physical ones. Some of us argue that those differences are not qualitatively unequal. Simon Baron-Cohen puts forward the theory that these differences come about because male and female brains are 'wired' differently. By this, he does not mean that our brains are different but that our brains are balanced differently in terms of an empathizing/systemizing scale. He suggests that the male brain is predominantly 'wired' for the understanding and building of systems, whilst the female brain is predominantly 'wired' for empathy. He goes on to argue that in its extreme and unbalanced form, the systems brain results in autism. This partly explains the gender dominance in autism, and also partly explains why boys are traditionally thought to be better at subjects such as science and maths, whilst girls are thought to be better at English and languages for example. If this is the case, then this helps to explain why women often think of voicing one's achievements as bragging and arrogance, whilst men are far less likely to attach those particular qualities to the activity. This has a huge impact on our ability to sell ourselves, according to our gender and may partly explain why in a predominantly female profession, most senior managers are male.

If we now view the typical FE situation as already described, then a dichotomy immediately becomes evident. The predominantly male senior managers operate according to their predominantly 'systems' brains, analytically exploring the system in order to understand and construct rules which govern its behaviour. However, the predominantly female additional support staff operate according to their predominantly 'empathetic' brains, which leads to an intuitive understanding of other people and the ability to treat them with care and sensitivity. If we, as additional support staff, are to communicate effectively with senior managers, then as well as communicating directly with them, we have to do it on their terms. This means that we have to provide them with an account of how we benefit the organization in a way in which they can recognize, analyse and systematize. Therefore we have to be clear, direct and confident in our approach, whilst at the same time being non-confrontational. This should not be a problem as these are all skills which are needed for working with autistic students in which you will be well practised.

Experience has shown that the following ways are effective for informing senior management of:

1. *Who you are*

    • Provide a breakdown of staff, in terms of their skills, qualifications, strengths and experience. Send it to senior managers and update it as new staff members join the team. This is quite common in the private sector, where a service is bought and can be sold to managers as advantageous for inspection.

    • Inform managers personally when staff gain new qualifications.

    • Inform managers personally when staff move on and invite them to the leaving celebration. They probably won't come, but they will have been kept informed.

    • Use existing in-house media, for example bulletins or intranet announcements to welcome new staff to the team and to celebrate success and achievements. Publicly acknowledge the loss of team members in the same way and celebrate their progression.

    • Make a team information board which includes photographs of all team members. Display it prominently in the college and on the website.

2. *What you do*

    • Produce information leaflets which outline all the services provided by the team and send one to each senior manager.

    • Use the existing college media to advertise the services of the team.

    • Contribute a page to the college website or design your own website. Send a link to senior managers.

3. *Why and how you do it*

    • Send an outline of staff training sessions to senior managers, together with an invitation for them to attend.

- Photocopy or produce your own information leaflets on good practice and send one to senior managers.

- Contribute to the wider debate and send copies to senior managers.

4. *What you achieve*

- Publicly announce and celebrate all students' and staff achievement.

- Organize an annual celebration of achievement and invite senior managers, influential people and members of the press to it.

- Publicly acknowledge any awards or accolades which the team receives.

- Inform senior managers when the team receives recognition and thanks from parents and students.

This may seem a daunting addition to an already heavy workload, but you will already be completing many of these tasks and you may also have initiated some creative methods of your own. This is not prescriptive but experience has demonstrated that these methods provide direct ways of communicating with senior managers in a way which raises the profile of the service you provide. One further tip would be to remember that people who have predominantly system brains are likely to prefer such forms of communication as tables, graphs, bar charts etc. These can minimize the effort and simplify updating the information.

Mainstream colleagues

I said earlier in this chapter that it is easier for support staff to raise their status with mainstream colleagues than it is with senior management. This is of course a huge generalization, and experiences will vary considerably between colleges, but also between departments within individual colleges. Attitudes towards support will have been formed, based on previous experiences and beliefs. This is part of the 'baggage' which we take with us in the evolution process of a specialist service. Many generic support teams operate from the basis that they support the student's learning. From this perspective, support staff are expected to support the lecturer in teaching the student. This often results in assisting with tasks which the lecturer has either not done, or does not want to do, such as photocopying or preparing materials, as well as supporting the student. This automatically defines the status of the support person as a 'helper' who is less skilled than the lecturer. The continuation then perpetuates this belief. If we are to provide a person-centred autism-specific support service, it is imperative that this perception is changed, so that support is directed by the needs of the student.

The first step in raising the professional status of support staff, is clarifying their role of supporting the autistic person. This must be made clear to all mainstream lecturers who teach the autistic students who receive support. Experience suggests that this should be given in a form of guidance to lecturers which is either provided or sanctioned by someone who has some level of managerial responsibility for student support. This clarifies at managerial level that the person who is providing the support is there to support the student, not the lecturer and that it should not be expected that they do anything which detracts from supporting the autistic student. Of course, this does not exclude them from being helpful people. If management does not provide the clarification, then I would advise that the person who is providing the support explains their role to the mainstream lecturer as soon as is practically possible. This will ensure that they do not have to justify their refusal to perform a task which takes them away from their responsibility of supporting an autistic student, at a later date. It will also constitute the second step towards raising their professional status, which is, being professional.

Earlier in this chapter, I implied that there is an issue because few support staff are employed on lecturer's contracts or the equivalent. I stated that this has an impact on staff recruitment and retention. It also has an impact on 'being professional'.

Professionalism is one of those words which is commonly used but rarely defined. It refers directly to the way in which we are seen to behave and it is assumed that everyone has a shared common understanding of it. The *Penguin English Dictionary* defines it as being fully trained and skilled, as opposed to being an amateur. In terms of supporting autistic students, it is related to being skilled and knowledgeable in our area of work, but it is far greater than the sum of those two things. In terms of working with autistic students, professionalism reflects the following factors:

1. A commitment to competence, in terms of specialist knowledge and practical skills.

2. A recognition and desire for continued personal and professional development.

3. A commitment to the application of principles, values and standards.

4. A commitment to personal integrity.

5. An acceptance of responsibility and accountability for one's actions.

6. A commitment to excellence and good practice.

7. Recognition of the need for objectivity.

8. A commitment to being person-centred.

Experience demonstrates that when support staff apply these eight factors to their work, then their job title and its associated status becomes irrelevant and mainstream colleagues cannot fail to recognize and value their skills and contribution to the teaching situation. (I will explore these factors further, later in the chapter.)

It seems appropriate here to emphasize that the need to regain professional status for support staff, is not simply to put them on an equal footing with mainstream lecturers, but to improve the service which we provide for autistic students. Raising the professional status of these positions, improves our practice because good professional practice includes developing and maintaining effective working relationships with our colleagues. If we follow the above eight factors we will do this. We will also increase staff morale and create positions which are attractive and desirable, which will have a positive knock-on effect for recruitment and staff retention. Issues relating to staff pay and working positions can then be tackled from a position of strength and equality.

The main reason that increasing our professional status is easier amongst mainstream colleagues is that they are presented with the evidence of our professionalism in a way that senior managers aren't, that is, face-to-face. They have a face-to-face relationship with support staff, and in this situation, our professionalism speaks for itself. More importantly however, they have face-to-face contact with the autistic students who we support. Most mainstream lecturers recognize that they cannot 'manage' autistic students, without this support. When they see the dramatic difference in terms of the academic progress and social behaviour, which autistic students experience, and observe the process of support first hand, they begin to recognize the skill and professionalism involved. However, there is a downside to this as we can become victims of our own success. The features of autism can be so subtle (especially when we get things right and provide a low arousal, well-supported environment), that unskilled people can be unaware of the need for continued input to maintain this balance. On a number of occasions I have had experience of mainstream lecturers suggesting, after only a short period of time, that support could be removed because it has achieved its desired outcome. This view arises out of ignorance, and there are a number of different ways of dealing with it. Again, experience suggests that it is more effective to take the professional route of extending the mainstream lecturer's knowledge of autism rather than the one of removing support to prove the point. This would be very effective but also extremely damaging for the autistic person and would not be in line with the eight factors of professionalism as outlined above.

I have indicated throughout this book that working with autistic people is a job for specialists, but I have also recognized that few FE colleges have the luxury of developing an autism service from scratch. Most ASC specialist services seem to have evolved out of an existing support service within the organization. Whether a service is created or has evolved is of no importance, as the strength of an ASC specialist support team lies in the quality of its team members. In fact, it could be said that the team is only as strong as its weakest member.

It is the responsibility of the team leader therefore to ensure that quality staff are recruited to the team.

Staff recruitment

The key to recruiting quality staff lies in understanding their role. Every aspect of the recruitment procedure, if properly followed, hinges on the job description. If the job description is not accurate, then it needs to be changed so that it more accurately reflects the specialist nature of the role. This can usually be done by adding relevant autism specific information to an existing generic framework. From the revised job description, a person specification should be drawn up which accurately reflects the qualities and skills which are essential and desirable for anyone to work with autistic people. This task needs a high level of knowledge and understanding of autism and experience suggests that it is where the potential for problems begins. Most job descriptions and person specifications are drawn up by managers or Human Resource personnel, who do not fully understand the nature of autism or the support which it requires, but who have a complete understanding of the structure and needs of the organization. As a consequence, job descriptions and person specifications are usually driven by the needs of the organization, not the needs of autistic people. If we are to provide a service of excellence which reflects good practice, then everything about it has to be autism specific and person-centred. This should include job descriptions and person specifications. This is not difficult to do, it just requires a different starting point. That starting point must be the needs of autistic people.

Different colleges employ people on different contracts and pay scales and it is right that employees should be protected from exploitation by employers. Job descriptions will therefore vary, according to the level of the position set by the organization in negotiation with the relevant trade unions. This makes it impossible for any book to provide specific instructions for job descriptions, but the process which underpins any ASC-specific job description and person specification should be the same, regardless of the point and pay scale at which people are appointed. I have found that following the process outlined in this chapter, helps to reduce the human error factor of the recruitment and selection process considerably.

The process underpinning recruitment

From an autism-specific person-centred perspective, the process must begin with:

1. Identifying the needs of autistic people

This can be achieved in the case where the person recruited is to work specifically with one student, by identifying their personal needs. In the case where the person recruited is to work with a number of unknown autistic students, it should identify the needs of autistic students based on the following:

- What autistic people tell us.

This can be gained from listening to autistic people or reading the works of writers such as:

Donna Williams
Temple Grandin
Claire Sainsbury
Luke Jackson
Liane Holliday Willey
and others.

- The study of academic theories and literature, particularly:

    ◦ The Triad of Impairments
    ◦ Theory of Mind
    ◦ Central Coherence Theory
    ◦ Dysexecutive Functioning Theory.

I would encourage you at this stage, to think of the children's song 'I can sing a rainbow', and practise listening with your eyes and other senses, as well as your ears. You will learn a great deal more.

2. Writing an autism-specific job description

This should be based first of all on the needs of autistic people as identified under point 1 above, followed by the eight factors of professionalism. It should then reflect the professional role as determined by the organization. Prior to leaving my position at The Sheffield College, I asked ASC specialist learner support assistants to contribute to a description of what their job involved. I have included the outline which they gave me, at the end of the chapter for interest.

3. Writing an autism-specific person specification

This should be based first of all, on the needs of autistic people as identified in point 1 above, followed by the eight factors of professionalism and the practical requirements of the specific position.

4. Advertising

This must be based on the autism-specific job description and person specification.

5. Short-listing

This should be based on the applicants' responses to the autism-specific job description and person specification.

6. Interviewing

Questions should be drawn up, which reflect the autism-specific job description and person specification and rated accordingly. In practice, it is well known that interviews are heavily biased towards people who have good interviewing technique, and that on their own, they are not always the best selection tool. Because of this, I favour a multi-method approach which involves autistic people in the decision-making process. In addition to the interview, presentations can be used to provide an opportunity for applicants to demonstrate their knowledge and understanding of both ASC and the requirement of the professional role. Confident autistic people should be involved in the selection process wherever possible. This would ensure that the correct questions are asked. It would also enable an assessment to be made of each applicant's ability to communicate with autistic people, as well as providing an indicator of their attitudes towards them and their ASC. Visits prior to the interview should be encouraged and valued.

It can be seen that the whole process of selection, in first of all identifying the needs of autistic people, is geared to ensuring as far as is possible that the person appointed has the skills which are relevant to working with autistic people. In addition, by including the eight factors of professionalism, it ensures that recruits will have a suitable attitude and approach to autism and support.

Experience of working with autistic people is not always an indicator of an applicant's ability to be 'professional'. Experience suggests that it is relatively easy to teach someone about autism, but it is very difficult to teach professionalism to a person who does not share a commitment to the values and attitudes which underpin what I have outlined as professionalism, when working with autistic people. In some ways, working with autistic people can be compared to driving a car in that once a driver has picked up bad habits and attitudes, it can be extremely difficult to remove them.

Identifying the needs of autistic people in terms of staff recruitment

Autistic people tell us that the right people, who have the right attitudes and approach, can make a huge difference to their educational experience and achievement. Whilst the nature of the professional role will dictate the tasks which direct the drawing up of the job descriptions, the personal qualities which an applicant requires to work with autistic people, will be constant across all professional roles. Autistic people indicate that the following qualities are essential for all staff who work with autistic people:

Essential qualities

- The ability to use a variety of different media and forms of communication.

- Creativity, intuition and sensitivity.

- Problem-solving skills.

- Empathy.

- The ability to be non-confrontational in approach.

- A positive view of autism.

- Resilience.

- Good listening skills.

- Patience and the ability to remain calm at all times.

- Knowledge and awareness of the individual nature of autism.

- To recognize behaviour as a form of communication.

Academic theories and literature indicate that the following additional qualities are essential:

- Clear and direct communication and social interaction skills.

- A good understanding of the role of non-verbal communication.

- Negotiation, interpretation and advocacy skills.

- The ability to use initiative and act on it.

- Good social skills.

- The ability to think on one's feet.

- Good organization skills.

- The ability to motivate students.

- The ability to apply theoretical knowledge in practical ways.

- The ability to work as part of a team.

- The ability to combine structure with flexibility.

In addition, it is essential that applicants are able to demonstrate that they are committed to a professional approach to support, as described in the eight factors of professionalism outlined earlier in this chapter.

Desirable qualities

I would suggest that the following qualities are desirable as opposed to essential:

- to be computer literate
- to have a current driving licence
- to be able to keep records and write reports
- to have good admin skills.

The interview

Interviewers are not necessarily good at interviewing. Despite training and guidelines which are intended to ensure that the selection process is fair and effective, mistakes are sometimes made which are regretted afterwards. I have been told by many of the people who I appointed at The Sheffield College that I have exacting standards, and that they found their interviews difficult and challenging. That does not surprise or embarrass me. It is my experience that the strength of the team depends on its individual members and it is important to get it right. It is possible to be kind and friendly when interviewing people whilst at the same time being rigorous and setting high standards. Providing that the early stages in the selection process have been geared to the requirements of the role, the applicants who are short-listed should be up to the task. Mistakes are sometimes made along the way, however. On one occasion, I interviewed an applicant whose application form was excellent, but who couldn't answer any of the interview questions. I found out during the interview that she had received significant help from her mother in writing her application, so it was not a true reflection of her ability and skills. If this happens, sensitivity and kindness have to be employed. It is not the function of the interview to destroy people, but good practice determines that standards should not be compromised. In my experience it is better for appointments not to be made if the applicants do not meet the desired standard.

Interview questions are not easy to set and considerable time should be devoted to this task. Sometimes, one question can provide information on more than one of the essential criteria, and these should be identified prior to the interview to ensure that all criteria are covered. A good interview should last for at least half to three-quarters of an hour and the candidate should do most of the talking. The structure of the interview should be made clear to the candidate at the outset, and an opportunity should be given for them to ask questions. There should be a time to put the candidate at ease by asking 'warm up' questions, and the remaining questions should be designed to encourage the candidate to talk, and to reveal their attitudes, values and principles, as well as their knowledge and skills. Questions can only do this if they are open. A mixture of question types should be used, including:

- What do you understand by? type of questions, which can demonstrate knowledge, and attitudes.

- Questions which present a scenario and ask the candidate to describe how they would deal with it. These demonstrate practical skills, initiative and attitudes, as well as demonstrating an understanding of the requirement of the role.

- Questions which ask the candidate to identify potential problems. These indicate sensitivity, social skills and self-awareness etc.

- Questions which ask the candidate to identify how they will benefit the team. These indicate the ability to work in a team.

- Questions which ask the candidate to draw on past experience to give examples of good practice. These types of questions ensure that the candidate is good at the job and not just at interviews.

> - Questions which ask how they approach certain tasks. These indicate personal qualities such as organizational skills and advocacy skills.

I am always amazed when candidates do not have any questions to ask at interview. I appreciate that sometimes all the information has already been given, but this is a significant opportunity for candidates to indicate their commitment and interest and enthusiasm in the job. Candidates' questions can also provide good indicators of where their priorities and interests lie. Questions about opportunities for staff development and training for instance say a lot about a person's desire to progress and their professionalism, whilst questions which relate to policies and principles can indicate underlying attitudes and values. They should never be seen as purely mechanical.

The importance of the accuracy of the selection procedure cannot be over-stressed. The selection is only the beginning. If mistakes are made at this stage, they will probably have to be lived with for a very long time. Rectifying them afterwards is a difficult, time-consuming, arduous and sometimes impossible task which is dealt with in the next chapter: Maintaining an Effective Specialist Team.

The self-defined role of the ASC Specialist Learner Support Assistant at The Sheffield College (December 2003)

1. To provide a professional and confidential support service at all times. This includes the provision of both academic and social support.

2. To act as interpreter and advocate.

3. To provide lecturers with relevant information on the individual effects of ASCs.

4. To work closely with personal tutors and lecturers to enable access to the curriculum at the appropriate level for the individual student.

5. To negotiate on behalf of students.

6. To provide ways of involving autistic students in their own decision making.

7. To provide advice for mainstream lecturers on 'autism-specific' methods of teaching and assessment.

8. To identify areas of possible independence for students and to provide strategies for achieving this.

9. To differentiate learning materials in an 'autism-specific' way.

10. To provide ongoing social skills instruction for autistic students.

11. To contribute to the development of packages of strategies which enable individual students to manage their own 'autistic behaviours'.

12. To assist ASC specialist lecturers in the development and delivery of autism-specific teaching packages.

13. To identify and sensitively correct students' inappropriate behaviours.

14. To contribute to student reviews.

15. To maintain records.

CHAPTER 4

Maintaining an Effective Specialist Team

The previous chapters of this book have focused predominantly on individuals, whether they are students or staff. Chapters 2 and 3 in particular, emphasize the need for individuals who work with autistic people to have a high level of specialist knowledge and skills. This may have given the impression that effective support depends entirely on the skills and knowledge of the individuals who provide that support. This of course is not the whole picture and support does not take place in isolation.

Most of the educational support which autistic people receive is delivered by individuals. It is a mistake however, to think that this does not require teamwork. Teamwork is essential in providing a service of equality for all autistic people. Without it, all we can provide is an ad hoc service which varies in type and quality for individuals who are autistic. This does not satisfy the needs of autistic people, the organization, or the people who are delivering the service. An effective service, even when it focuses on the individual needs of autistic people, is also required to satisfy the needs of the organization. Over 25 years of experience suggests that in providing for the needs of autistic people, we will produce results which also satisfy the needs of the organization, but it is also necessary to satisfy the needs of the individuals who provide the service. Very few people enjoy job satisfaction when working in isolation. In addition, the nature of this kind of work requires that we receive support, advice and encouragement from others who can identify with our situation. Autism support is very exacting and demanding. Without the support of colleagues, it is easy to feel as if we are out of our depth. This does not encourage effectiveness.

What is meant by effectiveness?

Effectiveness is essentially about being able to produce results. However, it is not only concerned with producing results, it is also concerned with being efficient. Because of this, effectiveness involves issues relating to cost and time, as well as quality and skill. Unfortunately, Further Education is now a business which is required to make a financial profit. This can lead to conflicting views about effectiveness, in terms of how results are measured. The conflict is essentially over the needs of our students, versus the needs of the organization. The focus of the conflict occurs in determining the standards which are used to measure results. Those of us who are engaged purely in providing for the needs of students, will view results in terms of our students' overall wellbeing, personal progress and achievement. For us, cost and time is secondary to the quality of our service and skills. Those of us who are engaged purely in providing for the needs of the organization will also be concerned with progress and achievement of students, but success will be measured by financial profit and balancing the budget. Students' progress and achievement is then viewed in terms of how it affects this. The overall result of these two extreme positions is that teaching and support staff are subjected to increasing demands on their time, effort and skill and their needs are ignored. Ironically, this then provides the arena for the expression of the conflict. Whilst I recognize that the reality of the situation requires a balance between the two opposing needs, it is not my purpose to put forward the needs of the organization. My purpose in this chapter is to look at effectiveness, from the perspective of the needs of an autistic person. From that perspective effectiveness of the ASC support team still relates to the ability to produce results, but results are measured purely in as far as how they fulfil the needs and desires of the autistic person. It is my view that in doing this, staff needs are also met.

Measuring results

If, as has been suggested in Chapter 2, we are person centred in our approach, then the measurements we use to determine our results must also be person centred. This means that they will be individual, although there will inevitably be some areas of cross commonality. The process of profiling described in Chapter 2 will have gathered and assessed information in terms of the needs and wants of the autistic person. These will have formed the basis for making recommendations which guide and inform practice. Evaluations will be made which guide the continuous repetition of this process. This will have involved setting aims and targets and will have established standards for measuring results, which may relate to personal and academic achievements.

Example 1: Anthony

Anthony is 21 years old; despite being intelligent, he gained no formal qualifications at school, but his main ambition is to go to university to study computing, which he excels at. This requires amongst other things, that he first of all passes GCSE Maths and English or their equivalent. Both present very real barriers for him, and in the past he has been directed onto basic skills courses in these subjects. Anthony has never successfully completed these courses because his frustration has led to unacceptable behaviour and attendance difficulties. As a result, his performance in these subjects has not progressed. He has received additional support from the college to help with this, but this has not been ASC specific. Anthony has now enrolled on a Pre Access to Higher Education Course in Computing and has requested ASC specialist support with this.

With regard to Maths, the assessment process indicates that Anthony has strong arithmetical skills but that geometry presents a real barrier to him, because of the differences he experiences in visual perception. He also has some hand–eye coordination difficulties. Geometry is however an essential component of the Maths course, so as a barrier, it can not be removed. In the past, the judgement has been made that because of this, Anthony will be unable to achieve and that he should not be accepted onto the course. In this instance, the barrier is overcome by assessing for scotopic sensitivity (Irlen syndrome); using assistive technology; negotiating exam concessions and providing technical tutorials which maximize Anthony's individual thinking and learning style. Anthony is also given one-to-one ASC specialist in-class support. Targets are set with Anthony for him to:

- be able to draw a variety of geometric shapes on a computer

- attend college every day for two weeks.

The initial result, against which the effectiveness of the support which Anthony has received in achieving his targets, may be:

- to draw a square to scale, on a computer and to label its measurements

- to receive a record of full attendance for two weeks.

These targets, along with similar ones in other areas, are then evaluated, reassessed and new targets are set, which move Anthony closer towards his overall aim of accessing university.

The example demonstrates how, if we focus our effectiveness onto the needs and wants of our students, and provide a service which satisfies these, we also satisfy the needs which are set by the organization. This example illustrates how issues which affect funding, such as achievement, progression and retention are then automatically met by our results. If however, our effectiveness is guided by the organizational requirements, rather than the student's needs, as was Anthony's previous experience then our results may not demonstrate the standard required by either the student or the organization. This also has an effect on staff needs. When dedication, hard work and effort result in successful achievements for our students, we reap rewards and job satisfaction. If our hard work and efforts are not rewarded satisfactorily, then the result is often experienced as failure, frustration and futility.

Anthony is only one student however, and effectiveness requires that we are able to demonstrate similar results and outcomes for all autistic students. This can only be achieved through effective teamwork.

Barriers to effective teamwork

In Chapter 3, I described how a rigorous selection process can help to ensure that all team members share the same values and standards of professionalism. This will contribute greatly to a shared sense of identity, vision and purpose. All teams are however, made up of individuals and it is right that team members should retain their individuality. Teams also operate differently according to many different situational and circumstantial factors. A great deal has been written on the dynamics of group work, and it is not the purpose of this chapter to explore this, or to suggest a particular style of leadership or management of the ASC specialist team. It is essential however, to emphasize that there is a need for all team members to work together to provide consistency of approach. There are a number of factors which can undermine this. It is easy to suggest that these are an issue for the team leader to deal with, but each team member has a responsibility to ensure that the following factors are avoided, if the team is to be effective:

- lack of awareness of a team vision and purpose

- lack of effective communication channels

- physical isolation

- time pressures

- work overload

- individual discontent

- lack of direction

- lack of support

- uncertainty of individual's roles

- lack of supervision

- unclear guidelines

- lack of training

- high staff turnover

- unequal distribution of work.

If you are a team leader, and you would like to address these issues, then the following are strategies which I have found helpful over the years, in avoiding these barriers:

1. Provide an induction which is separate from the college induction programme. It should include:

    - time with the team leader

    - an induction package which provides a mission statement, guidelines, tips and expectations for the development of good practice

    - two weeks' work shadowing with other team members

    - a suitable period of peer mentoring (length of which varies from person to person)

    - set times for evaluation of induction

    - set times for continued appraisal.

2. Arrange team meetings. At a minimum, these should be fortnightly. They should be used to develop cohesiveness within the team, by providing time to discuss:

    - team approach to individual problems

    - professional values, attitudes and behaviour

    - individual team members' contribution to team tasks

- development of the team

- team social events.

3.   Provide regular supervision sessions for all staff. These should not be used as opportunities to criticize, but provide opportunities for both parties to evaluate progress and discuss personal development.

4.   Provide regular training sessions for all staff (see next chapter).

5.   Use the terms 'we' and 'us' as often as possible.

6.   Encourage continuous discussion and learning. This can be achieved through encouraging people to study and gain specialist qualifications and by building up a 'library' of books which are accessible to team members.

So far, I have defined 'team' as the group of individuals who are employed to work specifically in an ASC specialist support team. This is however, a rather narrow view of the term. Autistic people are autistic in every area of their lives and need support across all areas, not only at college. In fact, it is often more common for autistic people, especially those who have a diagnosis of Asperger syndrome to require more social than academic support. If support at college conflicts with the support that the autistic person is receiving from elsewhere, then it is likely to be confusing for the autistic person in the short term, and not effective in the long term. The term 'team' in this context, should therefore be extended to include people other than those who are immediately employed in the role of support. Every autistic student will be supported by a team of people who include amongst others: parents; carers; siblings; mainstream lecturers and people from other agencies such as church, clubs, careers, counsellors etc. It has been my experience that unless there are excellent channels of communication in place, these can be a source of conflict and confusion.

Communicating with parents, carers and siblings

The ethos of FE is directly in conflict with involving students' parents and carers, to the degree in which it is necessary for the autistic person. In attempting to distinguish themselves from schools and foster a more adult and independent approach to learning, colleges often follow a support model which encourages the student to take control and responsibility for their own support. This stems from the belief that giving some control and responsibility to the student will encourage motivation and commitment to learning. This is of course a false view in that control and responsibility for support are both placed firmly in the hands of the organization. Also, motivation and commitment to learning are affected by many other issues other than control and responsibility for one's own support. Control and responsibility are difficult issue for most students who need support, but the nature of autism makes it extremely difficult and stressful for the autistic person. I have often heard it said that autistic people do not know what support they need, or that in fact, they do not recognize that they need any support at all. Whilst this may appear to be the case, it is not strictly true. Often, when asked, an autistic student may tell you that they do not experience any problems learning, or that they do not need support, whilst the opposite is apparently true. This is usually linked to a lack of awareness, or a failure to take the perceptual differences between neuro-typical and autistic thinking into account, when asking the question. This may be compounded by the lack of skills in the person who asks the question, so that either the wrong questions are asked, or the right question is asked wrongly. Experience teaches us that parents or carers can be invaluable sources of guidance and information in these instances.

Many parents of autistic children have known what their children need, but have had to fight for them to be given the appropriate support. Many of them have spent many hours at school explaining to teachers that their child is not naughty but that their behaviour is a direct response to the exposure anxiety which they are experiencing because of their autistic condition. Most parents of autistic children understand and communicate with their children better than anyone else. Despite this, they are often criticized for being 'over-protective' or 'over-supportive' and are continually told that professionals know better than they do, despite the fact that their experience has often been to the contrary. Of course there are some parents who are over-protective, or who don't have the necessary skills or education to support their children effectively and of course there are also some parents whose lifestyle does not allow for them to have the level of input which an autistic child requires. The fact remains that however skilled a parent appears to be, they will spend more time with their child, and will know them better than a professional whose time is limited by their professional role. Despite this, parents are often seen as being 'over-demanding', 'threatening', 'unrealistic' as well as over-protective. In one instance I have known a 15-year-old boy be taken into care and his father accused of 'damaging his education', because he was so vociferous in his demands for his son's school to provide ASC specialist support. I would like to be able to say that this only happens in schools and that colleges are different but unfortunately, this is not the case. If anything, the adult ethos of FE often promotes and encourages this view. There should not be this conflict between parents and professionals. Both are working in the best interests of the autistic person and it is much more effective, to work together, as partners.

Parents as partners

'A pupil or student can be very successful in his education (academic and social) only to go home at 3.20 p.m. and cause absolute havoc' (Hesmondhalgh and Breakey 2001, pp.74–75). Similarly, autistic students can have difficult times at college and take issues home with them which parents have to cope with in isolation. Both of these instances, and there are many, many more, highlight the need for good trust and communication between parents and the ASC team. FE however, presents challenges for this which are not so evident with younger children in the school system. One such challenge occurs over issues of confidentiality.

The right to confidentiality is a concept which must be taken very seriously and adhered to at all times, but people often misunderstand and take it literally, so that it comes to mean that everything concerning a person should be kept secret. In this way, I have seen information about a student kept secret from some staff and parents, when its disclosure would have been in the best interests of the autistic person. This is not to say that the diagnosis of autism automatically means that an individual's rights to confidentiality should be ignored, or that everything about that person, including their diagnosis should be disclosed to everyone.

Confidentiality is defined for such purposes as this, by the International Standards Organization as ensuring that information is accessible only to those authorized to have access to it. This clearly makes confidentiality an issue of authorization, rather than secrecy. The misinterpretation of confidentiality as secrecy has in my experience often undermined the trust and communication between parents and support staff, which is essential to an effective working partnership. Of course there are times when working with adults, when it is right to withhold information from parents. Whilst these situations may present a moral dilemma, it is not too difficult to judge the appropriate action, if the issue of confidentiality has been discussed with both the student and parents in advance and authorization of when to disclose has already been given. This can be seen in the following example, which briefly describes a situation where an agreement had been reached by both parties which defined the boundaries of disclosure in a way which excluded 'typical age appropriate behaviour'.

Example 2: Graham

Graham is a 19-year-old student who has a diagnosis of Asperger syndrome. His parents have disclosed a past history of inappropriate sexual behaviour. They have been working with him to develop strategies and put boundaries in place which will help him to manage this behaviour. Graham makes a very inappropriate sexual advance on a middle-aged receptionist, which involves touching. The incident is dealt with sensitively and Graham's parents are informed. Earlier in the week, Graham has been seen smoking with members of his peer group. This generated discussion amongst staff who decided that it would be an infringement of his right to confidentiality to inform his parents of this. Some weeks later at Graham's annual review, his parents stated that they suspected that he had been smoking. They were unhappy about this, but that as it was typically 'age appropriate behaviour', they would not have expected to be informed.

Communicating with parents

Experience teaches us that it is essential to communicate regularly with parents and carers, as what might be considered a minor detail can have enormous impact on an autistic person. For some students, regularly can mean every day whilst for others, it may be less frequent. It is essential to establish a pattern and a channel of communication at the outset of the parent/practitioner relationship. If this doesn't happen, then an alternative pattern usually develops which is that a communication channel is only opened when there are problems. Parents then only contact college when they are unhappy about something and vice versa. This is extremely negative and doesn't promote effective working relationships with either the parent or the student.

Appropriate methods of communicating can present challenges in FE in terms of confidentiality and independence, but this and the frequency of its use should be discussed in advance and reviewed regularly throughout the autistic person's time at college. What may be appropriate initially, may not be appropriate as the autistic person matures and different channels of communication may have to be sought and used.

I have seen Dictaphones used effectively, both in school and in FE. The advantage of these is that they are quick and immediate to use. Once people get used to talking on tape, they can work very effectively and can be useful tools in developing close working relationships with parents. The main problems encountered in using Dictaphones are that they are very visible and it may not always be possible to listen to a long message immediately. I have known instances when other students have been suspicious of their use and have raised questions about their purpose. This can be difficult to deal with whilst maintaining confidentiality. I have also known instances when a message has not been listened to early enough and staff have not been aware of potential problems as a result. Neither of these issues are insurmountable.

I have also seen note books/diaries used for this purpose. I have a personal distaste for these. My experience is that they are indiscreet, time-consuming for staff, undignified for the student, and provide opportunities for breaches in confidentiality. I would not encourage their use, especially in an age when email is so often available as a superior alternative.

In my experience, the telephone is one of the most effective channels of communication as it is two-sided and enables the avoidance of any misunderstanding. For this to be effective, it is essential that ground rules regarding use are clear, and that responsibility is given to one member of staff for the contact. Without these, it can be intrusive for both parties.

My personal preference is the telephone, with the Dictaphone as a second choice as both of these involve non-verbal aspects of speech, such as tone, pitch, pauses and intonation. Whichever channel is used, it is essential that the communication should be regular, and should focus on the positives. Without this, I have known autistic people to perceive the contact as 'telling tales' with the obvious negative connotations and in such instances, they have erased messages from Dictaphones and have torn pages out of notebooks. Support should not be about conflict and this should be avoided at all costs.

It is worth mentioning that communicating with parents should not only be about passing on information about what has happened. This may be useful and informative, but it does not include parents as members of the support team and it has no benefit for the autistic person or the support team. The purpose of communicating regularly with parents is to understand the autistic person better and to ensure consistency and the development of effective strategies for support. This will be of benefit to all three parties.

Other professionals as partners

As an FE practitioner, it was my experience that other professionals were far more difficult to work with effectively than parents. This view continues to be reinforced by other FE practitioners, whom I meet as I deliver training. From what people tell me, it seems that there is a resistance amongst FE practitioners to new or different ways of working. Some professions also have a history of being 'got at' and devalued politically. Teaching, along with social work, is one of these. When professions have been devalued over a period of time, the people who work in those professions become disenchanted, but they also become defensive. In this sort of situation, people can feel vulnerable to criticism and attack. The combination of resistance to new ways of working and defensiveness as a response to continuous attack is particularly relevant to the area of autism support. Autism, particularly when it is presented as Asperger syndrome, is still a relatively new condition, especially in FE as it is only in the last five years or so that those with the label have been obviously visible in the system. As a condition, it challenges many previously held methods and beliefs regarding learning disability and forces us to learn new methods and practices if we are to be effective. This requires a significant level of knowledge and understanding not only of the condition, but of how autistic people think and learn. It then requires that we apply this knowledge in a practical way to our profession. Most people, despite having expertise in other areas, do not have this level of specialist expertise and it is not reasonable to expect that they should. The solution to this is found in the provision of specialist support. In some instances, people have high levels of expertise in one area, for example their subject area, but their practical and professional expertise has become outdated. If this has happened, then practitioners can be particularly defensive about their situation. This is especially evident in practitioners who have been practising for many years with no real programme of professional development in place. When this occurs, then there can be a tension directed towards the support practitioner and professional relationships can be adversely affected.

Problems encountered

Partnership implies equality and is often difficult to achieve if the two partners do not share equal status and respect. In Chapter 3 it was suggested that a professional approach would lead to some equality of status for support practitioners. It also suggested that advance explanation of the role of the support worker, whether they are a specialist lecturer or a learner support assistant, would help to minimize potential misunderstandings and foster good working relationships. Despite this, problems still occur. It is my experience that when this happens, it is invariably linked to the insecurity of the mainstream practitioner. Insecurity tends to manifest itself as:

- concern that one's authority is being challenged

- concern that one's professional skills are being observed and criticized.

There is no easy answer to this, except that confrontation and conflict should be avoided. Anyone who has supported in another person's class will realize that this is a very privileged position which requires respect at all times. Most lecturers know their subjects well and most are dedicated to their profession and are genuinely concerned about the best interests of their students. As in any profession however, some people struggle to achieve the highest standards. Discretion and tact are essential qualities at these times. Only in extreme cases, when it is obvious that the lecturer is not coping, should the support staff exert any authority over the class, and then it should be handled sensitively and supportively. On occasions, support staff may have genuine concerns relating to the professionalism and good practice of others. My advice, based on 25 years of experience, would always be to discuss these with your line manager and discharge your responsibility to them. It is common practice in business that people of equal status in the hierarchy should discuss issues of concern. In this way, staff who are of a lower hierarchical status in one section of the organization are not expected to have to deal with potentially difficult situations which involve staff who have a higher hierarchical status in a different section of the organization. This recognition that there is power attached to status is not so explicitly reflected in many FE colleges, but such a system is worth encouraging. In this way, line managers will talk to line managers and there is a situation of equality.

The support role is not an easy one. It requires a high level of interpersonal skills and professionalism. A rigorous recruitment process is crucial if a team's effectiveness in this area is to be maintained. Experience suggests that even the most hostile of mainstream lecturers can be won over by a combination of professionalism and student's success.

Lack of specialist knowledge can lead to mainstream lecturers misunderstanding and devaluing the role of support. As has been described in the previous chapter, it sometimes happens that lecturers view improvement in student's achievement and behaviour as an indication that the student no longer needs support. Often, mainstream lecturers are also concerned that support may lead to dependency. Withdrawing support would very quickly indicate that this was not the case, but should never be considered with autistic students as the evidence indicates that it could have disastrous effects. It is far better for support staff to use their specialist knowledge, which is part of their professionalism and 'educate' the lecturer about the nature of ASC support. It is then usually possible to renegotiate an appropriate level of support. If a person-centred plan has been drawn up, the lecturer can be referred to this and a suggestion can be made that increased independence should be considered as part of the review process.

As always, experience shows that our students are our biggest advocates! Only on extremely rare occasions have I known a situation where a mainstream lecturer has worked with an autistic student who has been supported by an ASC specialist, where it has not been possible to overcome any hostility. Mainstream lecturers, however hostile, usually recognize achievement and progress and also recognize that it could not have been made without the support of ASC specialists. This has a huge impact on the future working relationship.

FE practitioners encounter a range of different professionals who work with autistic students. Most of the problems encountered with these professionals occur through a lack of communication and understanding of ASC. Most of them are beyond the control of an ASC specialist team, but I have hinted in the above discussion that there is a role for 'educating' in these situations. This will be discussed in the next chapter on staff training.

CHAPTER 5

Staff Training

In Chapter 2, I defended the view gained through experience, that specialist skills are needed to work with autistic people, and that it is possible for these to be found in mainstream settings. I also cited a report by the National Autistic Society (Barnard *et al.* 2002), which found that only 25 per cent of special schools considered that their teachers were adequately trained in working with autistic students. This view is supported by my own unpublished research, conducted in 2004, which also suggests that most FE practitioners who work with autistic people recognize that they need training in this area. A recent Learning and Skills Development Agency (LSDA) Disability Discrimination Project (Tarleton 2004), which focused on including autistic students in FE, identified that training for FE staff would enable them to empathize and understand autistic students, and also enable them to understand and manage autistic student's behaviour better, both in the classroom and in the wider college context. My experience as I visit FE colleges throughout the country is that staff are eager and hungry to learn but are dissatisfied, either with the lack of training, or with the type of training which is available to them. I am constantly told that 'anyone can provide information on the triad of impairments', but what staff want is what they call 'nitty gritty' training. By this, they mean training which addresses the issues which they face on a daily basis and provides practical suggestions and skills to deal with them.

In *Access and Inclusion for Children with Autistic Spectrum Disorders* (Hesmondhalgh and Breakey 2001), I said that there was very little 'autism-specific' training available and that what there is tends to be more academic than practical. A quick internet search would suggest that this is no longer the case as there are many independent agencies offering training in ASC. This raises questions as to why so many FE practitioners are dissatisfied with the training they have received. My research suggests the following:

1. The quality of the training is often adversely affected by the trainer's limited knowledge and practical experience of ASC.

2. The training is academic.

3. The training is part of a 'one size fits all' package and is not specifically relevant to FE or to the individual's professional roles.

4. The training does not have a practical application.

5. The training is 'outdated'.

Quality of training

Quality of training is directly linked to the quality and skills of the trainer and in the area of ASC, these vary enormously. It is relatively easy for anyone to set themselves up as a trainer, with or without the relevant qualifications and experience. I would recommend therefore that participants check out a trainer's credentials before booking them or attending any course. Time is precious and no one wants to waste their time attending a course which at best, is less than helpful and at worst is damaging. The LSDA report already mentioned recommends that trainers should:

• be knowledgeable regarding ASC and the current theories

• have detailed practical experience of working with autistic individuals in an educational setting, preferably FE

• be able to challenge pre-conceived ideas and stereotypes of ASC

• be able to see the difficulties faced by a variety of different staff

- be able to provide practical suggestions and strategies

- be aware of funding issues

- be willing to adapt materials so that they relate to the precise needs of the audience

and that training should always be:

- tailored to the needs of the specific group of staff and

- immediately relevant and responsive to the needs of the group at that time.

Following these recommendations will enable some screening of potential trainers but I would suggest that you also talk to the trainer in advance and ask questions about them and their courses. Many trainers fall into the 'one size fits all' category. They are not autism specialists and have a selection of packages on different areas of disability, which they deliver over and over again to a variety of audiences. This is not a foundation for quality training as it can only provide a very basic and general picture of whichever area of disability is being addressed. The starting point for any training session ought to be to establish who the audience is, where and how they work and what is their shared knowledge base. Without this information, no trainer, however skilled will be able to fulfil the guidelines outlined above. If the trainer does not ask questions about who is participating in the training session, then there is no possibility that he or she will be able to sufficiently address the needs of the group. I would also suggest that you ask questions about the trainer in advance, which disclose any preconceived ideas and negative stereotypes which the trainer may have. If the trainer has a website, this can provide a good way to find this out. Some people are however very good at selling themselves and at the end of the day, the product may bear no resemblance to the advertising. I have been on training courses where the trainer has represented autistic people in a negative light, not used inclusive language, and made jokes at the expense of autistic people as well as swearing in their delivery. This sort of behaviour is unacceptable. Evaluations should be part of all training sessions and these should be used to feed back such criticisms to the trainer and if appropriate to the organization which they are part of. It is often useful to ask to see a trainer's evaluation form before arranging an event, as this can indicate their personal values. If a trainer can not provide an evaluation form, then I would recommend that you avoid using them. One of the purposes of evaluation is to inform future practice. Without evaluations, no trainer can improve on their performance.

Who to train?

Training budgets are limited and the current approach to training in FE often seems to be, to send one or two delegates on a training course and then expect them to deliver the same training to a group of staff on their return. This may seem effective, but in my experience, this always results in quality being sacrificed for economy, and that this is a false economy.

It is extremely difficult, even for experienced trainers, to deliver effectively a training session which someone else has planned and prepared. It is virtually impossible to do this if you don't have access to the resources which were used as well as lacking specialist knowledge in the area concerned. It is inevitable that in this type of dissemination the 'message' will be diluted and possibly distorted and will certainly be far less effective. In addition, it is not really cost effective. A 'typical' training session from a recognized and reputable FE training provider, costs at the time of writing approximately £215.00 per person. Two delegates to such an event would therefore cost the college £430.00 plus the delegates' travelling expenses. The current daily rate for a trainer from a similar organisation to deliver a full day's training to 20 or 30 staff, at any college, costs between £450.00 and £850.00 plus expenses. This is a much more cost and quality effective method of training.

I indicated in Chapter 2 that it is not necessary for everyone who works in FE to be an autism specialist, as long as there was easy access to those who are. I also indicated that because autism affects every area of a person's life, everyone who has regular contact with autistic students whilst they are at college should be given ASC training. This is not a contradiction. I firmly believe that everyone who works in FE and comes into regular contact with autistic students should receive training in autism awareness. This should include librarians, receptionists, security and canteen staff, as well as teaching staff. This is a view which is supported and recommended by the Autism Manifesto put forward by the All Party Parliamentary Group on Autism, (APPGA) in 2003. 'There will be a statutory requirement that all professionals or auxiliary staff working with people with autism will have received autism awareness and job-specific training in autism prior to commencing their employment.' (APPGA 2003, p.1) There is also a strong argument to support the view that some students should receive autism awareness training, in order to operate a buddy type system of support. Attending one autism awareness course, however, does not make people autism specialists and the Autism Manifesto also recommends that there should be 'continued professional development'. There is a core of people in mainstream, to whom this particularly applies. These people, who work more closely with autistic students, should receive further training in the specific areas of autism support which are indicated in the following section. Providing that the LSDA's recommendations are followed in the planning and delivery, training for these groups of people should present no real problems.

The training

FE staff report that an additional problem in autism training is that there seems to be a body of opinion amongst senior managers which suggests that one autism awareness training session is considered to be sufficient. Practitioners themselves recognize that this is only the beginning and report that attending an autism awareness training session makes them acutely aware of the extent of the task and also of their own failings and the need for further training and development of skills. Autism is one of the most complex conditions that we come across in FE. Its range and diversity challenges all areas of our professional expertise. It is still however, a relatively new condition in terms of our knowledge and understanding and we have only recently started to listen to what autistic people themselves have to tell us. Until recently, society's expectations were very low for autistic people and they were segregated with no expectation that they should continue their education beyond the boundaries of the special school. The move towards integration in the 1990s and its subsequent increase in the numbers of autistic students attending mainstream schools has only impacted on FE colleges relatively recently. Because of this, there is a dearth of practical knowledge and skills relating to autism within FE. In addition, unlike schools, teaching qualifications have not always been a requirement in FE and many lecturers may not have studied the art of teaching. As a result, they may have the mistaken belief that the study of topics such as 'thinking and learning' are only relevant to early years or 'special needs' teaching. Knowledge and skills in these areas are essential to all teaching, but is particularly essential to teaching autistic students. Autism challenges us to be creative in our thinking and to question theories in order to 'think outside of the box'. Because of this, awareness of the condition alone is not sufficient to fully address and inform our practice. We still have a great deal to learn and a more in depth understanding with continued updating of skills is required. Autism awareness is just the starting point for that process.

A range of training should be provided, and it should include the following areas:

- autism awareness

- understanding autistic thinking and learning styles

- ASC-specific differentiation and reasonable adjustments

- teaching social skills.

This is supported by the LSDA report mentioned, which recommends that:

- All staff who come into contact with learners with ASC including college management, cleaners, reception staff as well as learners with ASC peers should have autism awareness training.

- In addition, support staff such as librarians, canteen staff etc should have training in understanding behaviour.

Subject tutors who work with learners with ASC should have additional training in:

- thinking, learning and understanding behaviour
- differentiation/assessment.

Support tutors for learners with ASC and learning support assistants should have additional training in:

- thinking, learning and understanding behaviour
- social skills
- differentiation/assessment.

An autism specialist team would require additional training in areas such as:

- teaching ASC self-awareness
- developing adult relationships
- understanding sexuality
- the 'hidden curriculum'
- developing a 'buddy system'
- legislative expectations and the need for 'reasonable adjustments'
- person-centred planning, assessments and profiling.

Suggested outlines for the essential components can be found at the end of this chapter. These can be used to advise and guide the development of a planned training programme if desired.

How to train

There is a culture which has grown up around staff training which encourages the view that training is something which is separate from work and in fact, often bears little relevance to our practice. In my experience, this encourages us to view training in a negative way. Sometimes, it is seen as a welcome respite and a day off from the daily grind of work, especially if it is away from the college and a good lunch is provided! Other times, it can be viewed as a waste of time, which adds to the stresses and difficulties of an already heavy workload. Sometimes, in these instances, especially when it is in-house, it provides an opportunity to take a well-earned day off in the form of a 'sickie'. Training should be none of these things. It should be integral to our work experience and practice, and it should excite, enthuse and invigorate us. As well as raising our self-esteem and expectations, it should enable us to perform better, and it should contribute to making life easier for us. To do this, it must have a practical application. It must also be positively encouraged, and supported in the workplace.

Training can be divided into two main categories: formal training and 'on the job training'. Both of these types of training can be provided either externally, or in-house. In practice, it is rare for external trainers to be involved in 'on the job' training, whilst formal training is usually provided by external trainers.

Formal training

Formal training should never be undertaken as an isolated event, but should always be part of an individual's professional development plan, which also includes supervision and 'on the job' training. Following the guidelines given in the earlier part of this chapter will enable:

- the accurate selection of staff to attend training
- the accurate selection of a suitable specialist trainer to deliver the training
- a suitable and relevant course content
- the development of an appropriate training programme
- the efficient use of the training budget.

The main difference between 'training' and 'teaching' is that training should always address practicalities and provide practical suggestions which can then be applied to our practice. Attendance at a training event should therefore cause us to question our current practice and reinforce and challenge different aspects of it. This requires us to reflect on what has been learnt. I would recommend that time is given for all staff who undertake training to discuss and assess the practical implications that the training has for their role (if this is not integral to the training course). They should also be given time to identify practical strategies which can be applied in practice, by the whole team. This can be in the form of a follow-up session in the case of group training or in a one-to-one supervision session with the team leader if individual training has been undertaken. From this, an action plan should be developed for the whole team, which enables the practical application of the training. This is far more effective than the 'typical' feedback from the training session which is often expected.

'On the job' training

My experience suggests that this is both an essential and effective form of staff training and that it takes place on two different levels, official and unofficial.

Official 'on the job' training occurs within a structured framework such as work shadowing, supervision and mentoring. It is of particular value in specialist teams where staff work at high levels of intensity with autistic students. Unofficial staff training is often not recognized as it is so embedded in daily practice. It takes place at individual and team levels, through unrecognized channels such as observation, discussion and example.

Peer mentoring as a form of staff training

The word 'mentor' comes from Homer's Greek classic, 'The Odyssey', where it represents the divine advice and protection given to Odysseus's son. Its contemporary meaning is 'experienced and trusted advisor' and its value is recognized in a variety of professions. In terms of FE, peer mentoring can be defined as the provision of guidance, advice and support given by a team member who is of a similar status but who is more experienced than the recipient.

Effective mentoring does not happen automatically but should be encouraged and developed as a scheme. There are a number of key points which should be considered in doing this as follows:

1. Mentoring should complement other training strategies.

2. The individual roles, objectives and expectations should be clearly defined.

3. There should be an evaluation process in place which informs future development and practice.

4. There must be good coordination and resources made available to both parties.

5. There should be a system of accountability.

Mentoring requires an ability to form effective one-to-one professional relationships. In addition to having good interpersonal skills and a high level of knowledge, skill and experience in the field of ASC, mentors should be non-judgemental and have the ability to analyse their observations and provide practical feedback in a positive and supportive way. They will need to be confident in their own skills, but also aware of their own limits so that they can ask for help when needed. Ideally, mentors should receive training in mentoring.

The benefits of mentoring are significant for both partners and the service provided. Mentoring provides a basis for sharing and developing skills, expertise and knowledge. It helps to increase self-esteem and professionalism in new team members which contributes to a sense of team identity. It recognizes and values experience and encourages established team members to increase their knowledge base as well as develop new skills which contribute to their professional development. Mentoring can be a way of problem solving and as such, contributes significantly to 'good practice'.

Work shadowing as a form of mentoring

I suggested in Chapter 4 that all new recruits should be given a two-week period of work shadowing as part of their team induction. This is something which I have always practised and found to be most effective as a quick training tool. I have only once experienced resistance to this, from a new member of staff who had previously worked in a similar but generic specialist environment. At the time, she did not recognize the need for shadowing, but the feedback at the end of the period was that the experience was invaluable as it demonstrated the ASC-specific nature of her new role. She is now one of the biggest advocates of work shadowing and is also one of the most effective mentors I know.

As in the advice given on mentoring, work shadowing:

1. should not replace other forms of training

2. requires the roles, objectives and purpose to be clearly defined from the beginning

3. should be evaluated at the end of the period

4. in addition, inexperienced and less knowledgeable staff should never be put in the position of being shadowed.

It has been my experience that non-ASC specialist managers have been confused about the purpose of work shadowing and have thought that it provided an opportunity for new staff to meet students who they may work with. Work shadowing has a training function in that the 'shadow' observes and learns from the experienced staff member. If used correctly, it provides a very effective form of initial 'on the job' training. New staff are often unaware of the intense level of engagement and continuous observation and assessment which is required in autism support. Work shadowing provides an opportunity to instil this practice at the very beginning of a new team member's employment.

Supervision as a form of staff training

The responsibility for supervision does not lie solely with the team leader or line manager. Every member of staff has a responsibility to ensure that they are adequately supervised. If you are not receiving supervision, then I would encourage you to raise this with your team leader as it is essential to monitoring your progress and development.

Individuals should also be proactive in identifying areas which require further development, and presenting them for discussion in planned supervision sessions. Team leaders should have the necessary knowledge and skills to provide one-to-one advice and guidance on these and they should also be aware of an individual's performance and skills so that they are able to identify any additional areas for development. Collectively, these can then be used to identify common areas for team training.

Supervision sessions should:

1. provide an opportunity for you and your supervisor to comment on your performance

2. provide an opportunity to identify and discuss your strengths

3. provide an opportunity for you to identify areas which you need to develop

4. provide practical tips and discussion of strategies for developing your performance, and

5. provide an opportunity for you to identify areas for future professional development and responsibilities.

Supervision sessions should not provide opportunities to gossip about other colleagues or to give or receive negative criticism. It is essential that it should be seen as a positive tool in enabling personal progression and development of knowledge and skills. Any problems relating to other work issues should be discussed at a more suitable time.

Discussion as a form of staff training

Informal discussion in the staffroom or sometimes in a more recreational environment, often provides the forum for intense discussion and debate about practice. As a team leader, my desk was located in the team staff room and I found that this contact enabled me to identify areas of potential concern as well as areas of great pride in my team members. Comments such as 'she can hear me, but she's just ignoring me', or 'he's such a liar!' can reveal a great deal about individuals' attitudes and practice. Similarly, our choice of language conveys a great deal about our inner feelings. Phrases such as 'suffering from autism' convey negativity and should never be allowed to continue, but they can provide unique opportunities for challenging inappropriate attitudes and teaching theory and skills. They also identify areas to target for further teaching and training.

I have also experienced literature reviews and the sharing of inspirational ideas and practice in the informal discussions which have taken place in the staffroom, or in my car. Autism practice is essentially extremely creative and it can be very difficult to come up with ideas on one's own. I regularly gave a colleague a lift to and from work for a period of about six years and these times were often the most inspirational. They produced some ideas for team working with students, in very difficult areas. I have included some of these in Chapter 7 on the 'hidden curriculum'.

Observation and example as a form of training

As the newly appointed Support Coordinator for autistic students at The Sheffield College, I was asked, rather cheekily, by a residential worker from a local special school: 'What training have you had to qualify you to do this job?' I was quite taken aback and replied along the lines that there wasn't really any specific training available for anyone in my position. I felt foolish afterwards as I considered myself well qualified for the role. I had worked with autistic people for about 15 years at that time, first of all as a qualified social worker and then as a qualified lecturer. I had a first degree in Communication Studies and I also had a Masters degree in the education of people with autism. Autism was (and still is) my passion and I had studied it avidly. Despite this academic study, I did not consider that I had received any formal training, as all of my training was gained through personal application of academic theory to my practice, supplemented by 'on the job' training. The 'on the job' training took the form of observation and example.

I have been privileged to work with some very skilled people in my professional life, one of whom is Matthew Hesmondhalgh, and I have learnt a great deal from observing and mirroring their practice. I remember in 1995, when I first started working with Matthew, being very challenged by the idea of working with one particular student whose behaviour was very unpredictable. I was literally quite scared of working with him because I was not confident that I would be able to 'manage' his behaviour and I was worried of 'failing'. I noticed that Matthew did not experience many of the difficulties with this student which other staff experienced, because he avoided direct confrontation and anticipated potentially difficult situations, defusing them whenever possible. In addition, he was always able to remain, or at least appear to remain, very calm in all his interactions with all of our students but most particularly with this person. I have always had the philosophy of 'if it works, use it', so when I worked with this student, I just copied what I had seen Matthew do, and it worked, so I continued to do it. Of course, it is now well documented that the use of indirect confrontation is essential in working with autistic people as is remaining calm at all times.

Over the years, I have noticed that this particular approach to training works well both in a specialist team and also in the mainstream classroom. Team members will notice that a colleague doesn't experience the difficulties which they experience with a student, and observe and mirror the actions of the more successful approach. This is a particularly effective method of in-house training, when there is an uneven status in relationships. It can be quite difficult for a support assistant to advise a lecturer on how best to work with a particular student as it appears to challenge their authority and skills which can lead to difficult working relationships. If however, the lecturer can observe that an alternative approach as demonstrated by the support assistant is successful, the result is often that they mirror that approach. Of course, this description is a bit simplistic and classroom relationships are much more complex than I have described them. In some instances, lecturers may observe the success of an approach but may not apply it to their own practice. In these instances, the visible success of the support assistant can be used as a springboard which enables them to tactfully explain their approach to the lecturer. This can then provide the opportunity for discussion of theory and practice. In some instances as a result of this, I have seen mainstream lecturers become interested in developing specialized skills in ASC and request more formal training.

Suggested outlines for training sessions

These outlines are provided to accompany this chapter. They are provided as examples which demonstrate the type of content which should be included in ASC training sessions for the areas which have been suggested as essential as all training should be specific for its purpose and audience, these outline are only suggestions and should not be used as set formats.

Autism Awareness: A One-Day Introduction Course

This one-day course has been designed for FE practitioners who are working with young autistic adults. It is suitable for staff who are new to this area of work, or who wish to develop their knowledge and skills in the area of ASC.

Aims

- To provide basic knowledge and awareness of the autism spectrum.
- To provide a framework for understanding autistic students.
- To provide practical strategies which can be utilized when working with autistic students.

Learning outcomes

By the end of the session, participants will:

1. have a basic understanding of the autism spectrum and how it impacts on individuals

2. be familiar with the main theories of ASC, which underpin good professional practice

3. recognize the need for an inclusive and person-centred approach when working with autistic students

4.   be equipped with basic skills which can be utilized when working with autistic students in the classroom situation.

5.   Content:

* Theories and explanations of ASC.

* Personal accounts, case studies and scenarios.

* A 'tool box' of classroom tips.

Teaching methods

Teaching will take place through:

* formal teaching

* small group discussions and feedback

* practical tasks based on case studies and scenarios.

Course evaluation

An evaluation form will be provided for each participant.

Understanding 'Autistic' Thinking, Learning and Behaviour

This one-day course has been designed for FE practitioners who are working with young autistic adults. It assumes prior knowledge and awareness of ASC and all participants should have first completed the one-day ASC awareness course. It is suitable for practitioners who wish to develop specialist skills for working with autistic students.

Participants will be required to bring examples from their experience to use during the session.

Aims

To explore and challenge the term 'challenging behaviour':

* to provide a framework for understanding 'challenging behaviour'

- to increase participants' understanding of the extent of 'difference' which autistic students experience in terms of their thinking and learning

- to understand the term 'ASC-specific'

- to provide practical ASC-specific strategies which can be utilized to reduce 'challenging behaviour' and improve communication and learning.

Learning outcomes

By the end of the session, participants will:

1. have increased their understanding of how ASC impacts on thinking and learning

2. understand what 'difference' means in terms of ASC

3. have an increased insight into behaviour as a form of communication

4. be able to utilize ASC-specific strategies to assist teaching and learning

5. utilize ASC-specific strategies to understand and minimize 'challenging' and 'disruptive' behaviour.

Content

- Relevant theories of thinking and learning.

- Traditional approaches to behaviour management.

- ASC perspective on behaviour.

- Personal accounts, case studies and scenarios.

- Sensory issues.

- A strategies 'tool box'.

Teaching methods

Teaching will take place through:

- formal teaching

- practical exercises and personal experience

- small group discussions and feedback

- practical tasks based on case studies and scenarios.

Course evaluation

An evaluation form will be provided for each participant.

ASC-Specific Differentiation and Assessment

This one-day workshop has been designed for FE practitioners who are working with young autistic adults. It is particularly suitable for practitioners who have already attended the 'thinking and learning' training, but will revisit elements of that course. It is also suitable for practitioners who have a basic knowledge and awareness of ASC and who wish to improve their skills with this particular group of students.

Participants may be required to bring examples of course work and forms of assessment to the workshop.

Aims

- To aid participants' compliance with current legislation when working with autistic students.

- To explore what the term 'reasonable adjustments' means when working with autistic students.

- To increase participants' understanding of the term 'ASC-specific'.

- To explore methods of ASC-specific differentiation and forms of assessment.

- To equip practitioners with ASC-specific practical skills in differentiation and assessment.

Learning outcomes

By the end of the session, participants will:

- understand the term 'ASC-specific'

- be able to apply current legislation to ASC

- have a clearer understanding of what constitutes 'reasonable adjustments' for autistic students

- have a clear framework for differentiating and assessing work for autistic students

- be able to utilize practical skills in ASC-specific differentiation and assessment.

Content

- Current legislation and codes of practice.

- ASC thinking and learning summary.

- Defining 'ASC-specific'.

- ASC differentiation and assessment.

- Practical application of theory to practice.

- Case studies.

Teaching methods

Teaching will take place through:

- formal teaching

- small group discussions and feedback

- practical tasks based on case studies and participants' examples of course work/assessments.

Course evaluation

An evaluation form will be provided for each participant.

Teaching Social Skills

This one-day workshop has been designed for FE practitioners who are working with young autistic adults. It assumes a high level of knowledge of ASC and it is essential for all participants to have first completed the one-day ASC awareness course. It is suitable for practitioners who work closely with young autistic adults and who wish to develop specialist skills in this area.

Participants will be required to prepare a confidential social skills profile of an autistic student, to bring to the session with them.

Aims

- To provide a framework for teaching social skills to autistic students.

- To equip practitioners with skills for assessing and delivering social skills teaching to autistic students.

Learning outcomes

By the end of the session, participants will:

- recognize the need for social skills teaching for autistic students

- be able to identify areas of social skills which may need specific teaching for the autistic person

- be able to design individual social skills packages for autistic students

- gain practical skills in delivering social skills teaching to autistic students.

Content

- Understanding communication and social behaviour.

- Linking theory to practice.

- Assessing for a profile of need.

- Teaching ASC self-awareness.

- Developing programmes of learning.

Teaching methods
Teaching will take place through:

- formal teaching

- small group discussions and feedback

- practical tasks based on students' profiles.

Course evaluation
An evaluation form will be provided for each participant.

CHAPTER 6

'Autistic Thinking' and the Need for Adjustments

The medical model of disability which was outlined in Chapter 1 has led to autism being defined as a disability which is characterized by deficits in the areas of communication, social interaction and imagination. This definition locates the 'problem' within the individual and measures the deficits against what is considered to be the neurologically typical 'norm'. This traditional way of viewing autism leads us to believe that autistic people are the same as their neuro-typical peers, but that they have something missing. This does not account for or explain many of the features of autism. In particular, it does not explain how a deficit can contribute to the original thought processes and outstanding achievements which some autistic people, particularly those who have a label of Asperger syndrome experience. Early biographical writings about autistic people encouraged this deficit view of autism. James Copeland (1972) records the hopelessness which parents felt in the 1950s and 1960s, when their child was diagnosed as autistic and the low expectations which they were encouraged to accept as realistic in the face of such insurmountable deficits. *For the Love of Ann* (Copeland 1972) documents how one child's parents refused to adopt this negative attitude and against all advice, challenged the opinions of professionals. This was one isolated case however, and it was not really until Donna Williams wrote *Nobody Nowhere* in the early 1990s, that neuro-typical people were given their first real insight into the mind of an autistic person through their own writing of their experience. Since then, such writings have allowed us to discover that the autistic person does not experience the world in an inferior way to those of us who are neuro-typical, but that their experience is qualitatively very different, and in many ways it can be seen to be of a far superior quality. Because of this, any understanding of autism should not be approached from a position of 'deficit', but rather from a position of 'difference'. Autistic people are not neuro-typical people with something missing or something extra added on. They are different. If we are serious about equality and inclusion within any area, then we must first of all understand that difference. It is common to approach the understanding of that difference through the Triad of Impairments, but I would argue that if we are truly serious about equality and inclusion, then we ought to have a different starting point and that starting point ought to be what autistic people tell us.

If we are serious about equality and inclusion, then we also have a responsibility to ensure that our practice does not discriminate against autistic people in any way. One way that we might unknowingly discriminate is by failing to recognize that autistic people, because of the nature of their disability, are placed at a substantial disadvantage when compared to their neuro-typical peers. In recognizing this, we also have a duty and a responsibility to make adjustments, which compensate for that disadvantage and put autistic people on an equal footing with their neuro-typical peers. This affects all areas of FE, from our admissions and exclusions policies, through to all the services which we provide, which includes our methods of teaching and assessment. This does not mean that autistic people are given carte blanche to behave in anti-social ways or that they will not be subject to the stringent academic standards which other students experience. What it does mean however, is that autism should not be used as an excuse for treating autistic students less favourably when compared with other students, with regard to these areas. It also means that we have to find reasonable means of addressing the balance for autistic students, in all the services which we provide. We cannot do this if we do not first of all fully understand the nature of the condition which requires us to make 'reasonable adjustments'.

What autistic people tell us about autism

Many autistic people do not experience autism as a 'problem' until they are told by neuro-typical people that it is. It is my experience that even those autistic people who have come to recognize and understand it from this perspective do not claim ownership of the 'problem'. I have been told many times by different autistic students that they do not have any problems; other people seem to have problems with them. I have also been told by autistic people that their autism isn't a problem for them and that if they were not autistic, they would not be able to excel in certain areas, as they do. Luke Jackson for instance refers to his autism as 'a gift' (Jackson 2002, p.19). It is not my intention to minimize the problems which autistic people experience on a daily basis but to emphasize that if we listen to what autistic people tell us about autism, then one of the first things that we learn is that even though they may describe a war, or a battle with autism, autism in itself, is not the problem. Their relationship with us and the environment is.

If we listen to what autistic people say and write, then as well as recognizing the individual experiences of autism, we can recognize that there are common themes running through what they tell us. Donna Williams uses the concept of to 'appear' and to 'be' (Williams 1996), whilst Liane Holliday Willey talks about 'pretending to be normal' (Willey 1999). Others refer to 'passing for normal' or 'trying to fit in'. Temple Grandin on the other hand talks about 'emerging' (Grandin and Scariano 1986). If we continue to listen, then we hear that trying to 'fit in' is extremely difficult and stressful. We also learn that despite considerable effort on their part, autistic people rarely fully succeed in this area and are regularly bullied, rejected and discriminated against, precisely because they do not 'fit in'.

Autistic people also tell us that they experiences differences in the way they process information, learn, think and feel. They tell us that they often have fascinations with things which other people find excessive or unusual. They tell us that they often experience high levels of anxiety and at times can be overwhelmed by their feelings to the point where they are unable to use their senses. They tell us that they often have difficulties in communicating with other people and that other people experience difficulties in communicating with them. They say that despite enjoying their own company, they often feel left out and unable to join in, to the extent where they feel like aliens from a different world to the one which they inhabit. They tell us that they think very differently from us, often describing it as 'thinking in pictures' or symbols.

Donna Williams, probably the most prolific autistic writer, whilst being careful to state that she is speaking from her own experience, has suggested that this is because autistic people experience difficulties in the areas of control, tolerance and connection. I have heard people dismiss these ideas as worthless, because they are only 'one person's experience'. My experience is that when I have explained autism to autistic people using this framework, they have all, without exception identified with her description and analysis. On occasions, autistic people have told me that even though they understood the Triad of Impairments, it was not until they viewed their autism from this perspective, that they truly understood their condition. Because of this, I have included it as the starting point for our understanding of autism.

Problems of control, tolerance and connection

Very basically, Donna Williams suggests that because autistic people have problems of connection, they also experience problems of control and tolerance. Connection is essentially to do with information processing, and most people are 'multi-track' as opposed to 'mono-track' in this area. Being multi-track enables people to process, monitor and access information consistently, through more than one sensory channel at a time. Most people can use all of their senses simultaneously, so they can make sense of what they can see whilst still hearing, and also experiencing the physical and the emotional. This enables them to be social. Most autistic people on the other hand are 'mono-track'; this means that they may not be able to simultaneously process, access and monitor the information which they receive through all of their senses, that is, make connections. For some autistic people this may be experienced as delayed connections, whilst for others, particularly those with the label of Asperger syndrome, connections may be made too quickly. Both of these are problematic and render 'social' as an elusive concept. They also lead to the use of involuntary compensations such as a temporary 'shut down' in one sensory channel in order to process information through a different sensory channel, or attention and avoidance strategies. In fact, most of the stereotypical behaviours associated with autism can be identified as compensatory strategies for the difficulties experienced by autistic people in making connections.

Problems of connection lead in turn to problems of tolerance, which can be either in the area of the emotions or the senses. There are other instances when people may experience emotional and sensory hyper-sensitivity, but Donna Williams suggests that when they occur together with problems of connection, then the result can be assumed to be caused by information overload. Intense sensory experiences can lead to captivation or avoidance. It is important to emphasize that sensory hyper-sensitivity is not only about bombardment, but involves an increased and heightened function of the senses. When the sensory experience is so intense, it can make it very difficult for the autistic person to function at any level. Removal of the stimuli will bring relief, but when this is not possible, the autistic person may use their own calming strategies such as rocking, tapping or humming.

Tolerance of emotion is experienced in a similar way, especially when it is linked to 'hyper-saturation'. Emotion is experienced physically and as such, has a sensory component to it. Emotions are therefore subject to the same processing, accessing and monitoring difficulties as sensory information. When emotional experiences are not made sense of, the result on the body can be so extreme that the autistic person may be overwhelmed by them and experience emotional overload or 'hyper-saturation'. As in sensory overload, this can lead to the autistic person switching to a subconscious level of functioning (autopilot) of which they are unaware, or systems 'shut down'. This could be as extreme as the inability to process any information for meaning, speech, movement or vision.

Problems of connection also lead to problems in control which can be the root cause of compulsions, obsessions and acute anxiety. Information needs to be processed at a deeper level than meaning for it to have effect. Donna Williams refers to this as processed for 'significance' (Williams 1996). On the rare occasions when autistic people are able to process information for 'significance', the repeating of the process provides the only significance (control) experienced in the lives of the autistic person. From this perspective, compulsions and obsessions appear to be problematic for the autistic person, whilst in fact the root cause of their difficulty is to do with information processing. Williams suggests that compulsions and obsessions should not be viewed negatively and attract imposed control, but should be used as bridges or motivational forces, to share and develop interests and improve processing skills.

I have found that viewing autism through this 'autistic perspective' explains it in a much more meaningful way than other theoretical perspectives are able to do. It also provides many more practical solutions which will be discussed later in this chapter.

I said at the beginning of this chapter that it is common to approach our understanding of autism through the Triad of Impairments but that it was my view that what autistic people tell us should provide the starting point. This is not to devalue theoretical study but to recognize that autistic people have precedence of expertise in this area. Good practice requires knowledge of both academic theory and personal accounts. There are three academic theories which I consider as a basic starting point in the knowledge and understanding of autism which is essential for our good practice. The Triad of Impairments is the first of these.

The Triad of Impairments

I wrote in an essay in 1996, that I considered the Triad of Impairments to be the pivotal point in our understanding of autism. I stand by that opinion. It wasn't until 1979, when Lorna Wing and Judy Gould conducted a study in Camberwell, South London that it was realized that Kanner's autism and Asperger syndrome are part of a wide range of conditions which have certain features in common. This led to the notion of the Triad of Impairments, which now informs all autism diagnoses. According to this view, autism is characterized by impairments in three areas of neurological development as follows:

1. *Social communication*

This refers to the use and understanding of verbal and non-verbal communication and can include:

- echolalia – repeating words and phrases
- missing out link words in sentences
- giving too much detail
- pedantic speech
- apparent difficulties with volume control – either too loud or too soft
- apparent difficulties with intonation – monotonous and mechanical speech
- literal interpretation of language
- confusion between sounds
- apparent difficulties using and understanding ambiguities and humour
- over-enunciating words
- using the wrong words.

In terms of non-verbal communication, the autistic person may experience difficulties in using and understanding:

- gestures
- eye movements
- facial expressions
- prosody (non-verbal aspects of speech)
- interpersonal space
- touch.

2. Social interaction

This literally means acting on each other or reciprocal action. Autistic people may appear to experience the following difficulties:

- apparent lack of awareness of the existence of others
- using little or no eye contact
- staring too long at others
- unresponsiveness when spoken to
- lacking in facial responsiveness
- avoiding touch and cuddles
- touching or hugging too hard
- remaining aloof
- social isolation
- excessive social gregariousness
- apparent formal and stilted behaviour
- aggressive or 'over-emotional' reactions.

3. Imagination

This is usually described as an impaired ability to produce ideas, especially mental images of what is not present or experienced. Autistic people appear to have:

- a lack of imaginative play
- obsessional, ritualistic behaviours
- a preoccupation with a limited range of interests
- difficulty in generalizing concepts from one area to another
- difficulty in problem solving and creative thinking.

In addition to this triad of behaviours, stereotypical repetitive behaviour patterns and resistance to change in routine are often characteristic. These may include:

- tasting, smelling, feeling or tapping different surfaces
- listening to mechanical noises such as washing machines
- switching lights on and off
- spinning objects
- head banging
- complex sequences of bodily movements
- lining up objects
- extensive routines and rituals
- attachment to strange objects
- collecting strange objects
- fascinations with numbers or sequences.

From the perspective of the social model of disability, the Triad of Impairments, is a useful tool for diagnosing autism and describing the areas of impairment. It identifies the symptoms of autism, but it stops short because it does nothing to identify the barriers within society which disable autistic people. It locates the source of the 'problem' firmly in the autistic person in terms of their skills and behaviour but does not contribute to our understanding of the 'what, why and how' of autism. It does not tell us what autism is, nor does it in itself really provide any practical tools for practice, although it does suggest areas for targeting support.

From the perspective of the medical model of disability, by which autism has traditionally been viewed, the Triad of Impairments is still a useful tool for diagnosing autism and describing the areas of impairment, but it takes on negative connotations. Because it does not make a distinction between impairment and disability, it encourages the view that the impairments or symptoms which it identifies are in themselves the disability. In this way, the symptoms become the condition so that the label of autism refers to the outer behaviour of the person, when in fact the condition of autism is to do with their inner reality. The outer behaviour, as identified in the Triad is then measured against the behaviour of the non-disabled population and is found to be lacking. In this way, it perpetuates the view that it is the possession of the impairments/condition which is disabling. The representation of the 'Triad' as an equilateral triangle also has negative connotations; it unintentionally encourages us to view autism as a fixed entity with equal distribution of impairments in all three areas. This has unfortunately led to many misunderstandings over diagnoses by less well informed practitioners and also to low expectations and aspirations for autistic people, in many professionals. The Triad of Impairments also does not account for the now well recognized differences in sensory perception which is the experience of many autistic people.

Theory of Mind (TOM)

'Theory of Mind' (TOM) is a relatively new concept which originated in the work of Piaget in the 1950s. The central feature of Piaget's work is the development of schemata. A schema is a hypothetical mental structure which contains all the ideas, memories and information relating to what we know about a particular thing. People develop schema through a process of assimilation and accommodation, which occurs through our interactions with the outside world, which Piaget calls 'operations'. Piaget suggested that there are four stages of cognitive development which enable us to perform different types of 'operations'. In this way, an older child is able to perform types of 'operations' which a younger child is unable to perform. Piaget suggests that each of these stages has certain characteristics. In the first stage from about birth to one and a half years old, Piaget says that the young child is 'egocentric'. This means that they have little or no awareness of anything outside of themselves. At this time, the 'self' or the 'ego' is the centre of everything and the very young child will consider anything which they come into contact with as part of themselves. Piaget suggests that children gradually come to realize, through their interactions with others, that there is a world outside of themselves, which exists whether they are interacting with it or not. Piaget further suggests that this egocentricity is one of the main features of a child's early years, but that it gradually reduces, so that by the age of about seven years old, it will almost be gone. By this stage, children are able to use their schemata to interpret and make sense of the world, although they will be unable to deal with abstract concepts until a later stage in their development.

In terms of autism, it is often recognized that autistic people appear to be 'egocentric'. Phrases such as 'selfish' or 'self-centred' are often used to describe this. In 1985, Baron-Cohen, Leslie and Frith put forward the view that this was because they lacked a Theory of Mind. Baron-Cohen (2000) describes TOM as possessing the ability to infer the full range of mental states which cause actions. These mental states include such things as imaginations, desires, emotions etc. TOM requires individuals to be able to recognize and reflect on what is in their own mind and the mind of others. Understanding the mental states of others allows us to make sense of their past behaviour, affect an impact on their current behaviour and predict (within limits) their future behaviour. These abilities are crucial in our interactions with others and in our performance of social skills. It is now thought that children develop a Theory of Mind at around the age of four.

Baron-Cohen *et al.* (1985) suggested that autistic people have not developed a TOM and are therefore unable to infer the mental states of others. They suggested that this was a kind of 'mind blindness' which made it difficult for autistic people to engage in human interactions for reasons which I have explained above. They are not therefore 'selfish', 'self-centred' or 'uncaring' but only appear to be so. This has important implications for the development of empathy.

Baron-Cohen et al's research (1985) was based on a false belief task which has become known as 'The Sally Anne experiment'. Very simply, researchers used two dolls; one called Sally and one called Anne, and acted out the following scenario with them: Sally placed a marble in her basket and then left the scene. When she was away, Anne took Sally's marble out of the basket and put it in her own box. When Sally returned, the researcher asked the child the critical question 'Where will Sally look for her marble? The correct answer is of course 'in her basket'. The experiment ascertained whether the child is able to take Sally's false belief into account. In other words, was the child able to mind-read Sally?

The experiment was conducted with a group of 61 pre-school children, 20 of whom were autistic, 14 of whom had Down's syndrome and 27 were described as of 'normal development'. The results confirmed that almost all of the 'normally developing' children and about 95 per cent of the children with Down's syndrome were able to give the correct answer. This compared with only 20 per cent of autistic children. These results were interpreted to support the view that autistic children fail to employ TOM.

This research sparked a great deal of further research, some which supports and some which refutes the original conclusion. Whichever view one takes, it is generally agreed that the TOM argument does help us to understand the nature of some of the impairments which autistic people have, but there are recognized features of autism which neither the Triad nor TOM addresses. In particular, because both approach autism from a negative position of 'lack of' they fail to explain the more positive aspects of autism for example:

- exceptional ability in certain areas

- excellent rote memory

- specialized knowledge and interests.

It is worth emphasizing that the 'false belief' test outlined above was conducted on very young children and that there were 20 per cent of autistic children who were judged to have completed the task successfully. This raises questions about the usefulness of the theory. It is possible to criticize this study from many positions for example, wooden dolls don't have mental states, and perhaps some of the autistic children's development of TOM was delayed. My reason for including it here is that despite its criticisms, TOM does have useful implications for practice.

Practitioners often tell me that one of the aspects of working with autistic people (especially those who have been given the label of Asperger syndrome), which they find most difficult, is their apparent selfishness, arrogance and lack of empathy. If TOM does nothing else, it helps us to understand that if the autistic person appears to be all of these things, then it is not through their intent, but is possibly a feature of their condition. This allows us to interpret the autistic person's behaviour differently and view it from a more positive perspective. This in turn has a positive impact on our practice.

Central Coherence Theory

Central Coherence Theory (Frith 1989) does not focus on the impairments or the deficits which characterize autism, but proposes that the mixture of assets and deficits in autism can be explained from an information processing perspective. Uta Frith suggests that this difference is one of weak central coherence. Neuro-typical processing, in an attempt to make sense of the information which is received through the senses, has a tendency towards viewing the 'whole' as opposed to viewing the individual parts. This is 'coherence'. Frith suggests that this tendency towards coherence is weaker in autistic people and results in a characteristic preference for processing the individual parts over the whole. This means that the autistic person focuses on the detail, which reduces the influence of any context on the information which they receive.

This theory suggests that rather than experiencing deficits or impairments, the autistic person experiences a difference in cognitive processing. The tendency to process information in a fragmented way, devoid of context explains the apparent impairments in communication, social interaction and imagination, which the Triad of Impairments identifies. It also explains the apparent difficulties which autistic people may experience in reading mental states (TOM). The real strength of Central Coherence Theory however, is that in addition to explaining the characteristic impairments and deficits, it also offers explanations for the more positive features of autism. The preference for processing the individual components of incoming information as opposed to the whole explains why some autistic people are able to excel in specific areas and rise to positions of eminence, where they are able to perform with outstanding success, whilst at the same time experiencing what others may term 'social incompetence'. It also explains the characteristics of perseverance and single-mindedness, which are invaluable components of original thought and creativity.

Unlike the Triad of Impairments and TOM, Central Coherence Theory does not view autism as a 'problem' which an individual has, but as a 'difference' which can be understood. It does not make qualitative judgements about the nature of the 'difference' and recognizes that these may have both negative and positive implications for the individual. As a result it presents autism in a way which is entirely compatible with what autistic people themselves tell us.

The need for 'reasonable adjustments'

In the UK, it is unlawful for colleges (or employers) to treat any disabled person less favourably than a non-disabled person, because of their disability. Currently, a student in FE is defined as being disabled if 'he or she has a physical or mental impairment that has a substantial and long-term adverse effect on his or her ability to carry out normal day-to-day activities' (The Disability Discrimination Act 1995 Part 4). This definition includes autism spectrum conditions (ASCs). When a person is placed at a substantial disadvantage by virtue of their disability, then it is expected that 'reasonable adjustments' be made. It is important to emphasize that 'reasonable adjustments' should remove the disadvantage which autistic students experience, not increase their advantage over their neuro-typical peers. In doing this, they compensate for the impairments which an autistic person may have and put them on an equal footing with their non-autistic peers. They are comparable with providing ramps and wide doors for wheelchair users, Braille reading materials for blind students and translators for British Sign Language (BSL) users. The theories and personal accounts outlined in the first half of this chapter help to identify the areas where reasonable adjustments should be made for autistic people. The rest of this chapter gives examples of the types of adjustments which it is reasonable for practitioners and organizations to make in the provision of services to autistic people. They fall broadly into two categories: those adjustments which should be made to the environment, and those adjustments which should be made to our practice.

Environmental adjustments

It is now widely recognized that autistic people's sensory experiences may be different from those of neuro-typical people. Donna Williams refers to this as sensory hyper-sensitivity. It is also now widely recognized that sensory stimuli can produce a heightened state of arousal in autistic people, which can culminate in what some autistic people term 'shut down'. This describes the emotional and physical state of collapse which occurs, due to the overloading of incoming information, rather like a computer crash. Reasonable adjustments should be made to the environment to take these sensory issues into account.

The individual nature of autism means that each autistic person may react differently to sensory stimulation and overload. Building design accommodates the needs of the group and has to take the needs of many competing factors into account. Only in rare instances is it possible to design 'autism friendly' buildings and even then the guidelines for these are usually provided by neuro-typical people who think that they know what is best. As a result, the reality for most autistic people is that they have to conduct their lives in environments which bombard and offend their senses. Many practitioners take the 'realistic' view that autistic people have to live in the real world, so the solution to their problems of sensory overload lies in 'desensitization'. In other words, they have to get used to it. If we apply this view to the area of physical disability, then it becomes transparently discriminatory and unacceptable. No one would suggest that physically disabled people should 'get on with' climbing stairs or question whether a building should have ramps and lifts to accommodate the needs of wheelchair users. In the same way, we should not suggest that buildings should not attempt to accommodate autistic users.

It is wrong to start with the assumption that FE colleges are not 'autism friendly' places and that changing them would be impractical and costly. Most FE college buildings are not in themselves inherently 'unfriendly' to autistic people, although they may have 'unfriendly' features and uses. It is also wrong to assume that reasonable adjustments to the environment can only be made through making alterations to the buildings. These assumptions, when they are made, encourage the view that the making of 'reasonable adjustments' in this area is immense and consequently impossible. They then inevitably result in defeatism and inaction. If we start from the assumption that our buildings already have some autism friendly features, for example neutral colours, and take the view that adjustments to the environment can sometimes be found in sources other than the building itself, then the task of providing reasonable adjustments becomes much easier as can be seen below:

1. Sensitivity to noise can present difficulties for the autistic student in many situations in and out of the classroom. Noisy clocks, lighting, heating, equipment and people, present real challenges, particularly when they are experienced in combination. Solutions can be sought in the replacement and redesign of noisy features, but these can be expensive and sometimes difficult to negotiate. Sometimes it is possible to soften noise by carpeting noisy areas and making alterations to the furniture, which reduces some noise, but more major alterations are not always immediately possible. In addition, there is some evidence from autistic people, which suggests that their hearing exceeds the normal range. This together with the fact that some noise is unavoidable suggests that solutions should also be sought from other sources. Many autistic people report that the use of ear plugs or ear muffs can be effective in reducing noise. Listening to suitable sounds or music on a personal stereo can also have a minimizing effect on auditory over-stimulation. Noisy places such as dining rooms should be avoided and alternative eating places should be provided. Alternative routes through noisy parts of the building should be identified or created and their use encouraged. Policies which prevent any of the above should be challenged and renegotiated. Other solutions can be found by adjusting our practice.

2. Visual over-stimulation can occur for a number of reasons. Poor artificial lighting, bright sunlight or fluorescent strip lighting are often potential problem areas. Brightly patterned aspects of a room such as wall displays can also have a stimulatory effect which may lead to sensory overload, and

stripes and grid patterns can lead to problems with coherence. Bright or shiny teaching materials can also be highly stimulatory. Solutions can be sought in refurbishment of the building and the installation of fittings such as daylight strip lighting, but alternative adjustments can be quickly and effectively made such as: requesting a change of room; arranging the wall displays so that the they are not in the line of vision of the autistic person, utilizing existing blinds or sitting the student so that they are turned away from glaring sunlight; allowing the student to wear sunglasses or testing for coloured lenses and altering teaching materials and including coloured paper for the autistic student.

3.   Smells can be a source of great distress because of hyper-sensitivity. Known areas of difficulty should be avoided wherever possible. Alternative toilet arrangements should be negotiated if needed and requests to change classrooms made whenever necessary. It would not be unreasonable or out of place for all students to wear nose and face masks in science laboratories if the smell is offensive. Other sources of smells such as the use of cleaning products might be more problematic to remove but should be challenged and a change suggested. The use of perfume will be discussed in the next section as part of adjustments to practice.

4.   Clear signing of the building is essential for autistic students. It is probably not age appropriate for these to be pictorial, but they could be symbolic representations. Alternatively, floors, departments and rooms could be colour-coded. This can be reflected in the student's timetable to aid their independence.

5.   Defining space within the classroom so that autistic students can work in an uncluttered place, away from the centre of the classroom, with minimal distractions would contribute significantly to a low arousal environment.

Adjustment to practice

In order to adjust our practice so that it does not disadvantage autistic students, we must first of all identify the areas where autistic students are disadvantaged. These are:

- during transition from school to college, and college to work

- in our admissions and exclusions policies

- by our timetabling

- by our lack of staff training

- by the lack of provision of specialist support

- in the arranging of outings and trips

- by the lack of provision of equipment and resources

- in the organization of work placement provision

- by the lack of provision of specialist advice services

- by our teaching methods and practices

- in the curriculum.

1. Transition

In *Access and Inclusion for Children with Autistic Spectrum Disorders* (Hesmondhalgh and Breakey 2001), I described the experience of the first two students at the ASC specialist Post-16 provision at The Sheffield College, in terms of their pre-access preparation and the initial difficulties which they encountered. These resulted in adjustments being made, which minimized the effects of their experience on their disability. This was an unofficial period of 'transition' which I described as 'progression'. Such a period of transition is a 'reasonable adjustment' which addresses the balance between autistic students and their neuro-typical peers. Many autistic students fail to access FE because of the lack of such provision.

Autism is a 'hidden disability', the manifestations and the severity of which are greatly affected by what the autistic person experiences.

Because of this, it is not always possible to anticipate the degree to which an autistic person may be affected by moving from school to college. It is easy to underestimate the effect which change has on a person when they have been in the same environment for four or five years, but as professionals in the field, we have a responsibility to anticipate potential difficulties and accommodate them.

When it is not possible to plan individual transition programmes in advance of the student's admission to college, an initial period of time will need to be set aside for this. The impact which autism has on people is very individual. It is therefore also not possible to prescribe a transition programme which can be used with every autistic student. Some autistic students appear to drop into college 'without a ripple', whilst others need an extended period of time to adapt to the new environment. My experience suggests that the first of these examples is a false impression. Usually, when an autistic student appears to need no special transition arrangements, it is because they have developed very effective strategies for 'pretending' that everything is OK, when in fact they are functioning in 'shut down' mode, or on 'automatic pilot'. Difficulties often become apparent much later, which are then far more difficult to remedy. Where there has been little prior involvement with the school or the student's parents or carers, then any transition programme can only be based in general knowledge and experience of autism.

General knowledge and experience of autism suggests the following in relation to transition:

- What works for one autistic student may not work for other autistic students so any transition programme will need to be individual to meet the needs of individual students.

- The period of transition should be formalized and a time should be set for its review. This way the aim to progress can be given in advance and the student can see transition as part of their overall programme of study. This helps to avoid a rigid expectation that it should continue beyond its usefulness.

- The transition period may require an individual timetable and curriculum. I would recommend that a social skills lesson and a homework session should be timetabled at this stage to avoid potential difficulties with rigid expectations.

- In certain instances, the autistic student may require a programme of individual teaching to ease them into the new learning experience (this is described in the individual accounts in Chapter 8).

- It is useful for autistic students to have a familiar person to assist them through the transition period. This person should be skilled in the area of ASC specialist support, and can either have been introduced to the autistic student in advance or could be someone from their school. New people can be introduced alongside these and the familiar person can be gradually phased out.

- The autistic person will need to be given clear explanations of what to expect in advance. Social Stories™ or cartoons (Gray 1994) can be useful tools for this.

- The transition programme should be flexible enough to accommodate any changes which the autistic student indicates as necessary.

- The transition programme will require some management of the environment. This can be in the form of physical aids such as ear plugs or dark glasses, or can be in the form of providing frequent breaks or time out, depending on the needs of the student.

- The transition programme should establish and use a regular channel of communication with the student's parents or carers whenever possible.

Often I am told by professionals whom I meet during training sessions that the provision of ASC specialist support in FE and at university is not doing autistic people any favours. The reason that is always given for this is 'when they get out into the real world, they will not be able to cope' or 'the real world isn't like that'. These people never have a satisfactory answer when I ask them what we should do. The answer is quite simple: we are either defeated, and take the view that autistic people are not going to cope in the 'real world', therefore there is no point in our attempting to remove the disadvantages which they experience in FE, or we take the view that as we are successful in removing the disadvantages which autistic people experience in FE, so we can be successful in removing those disadvantages that exist in the 'real world'. Transition from college to work is part of this challenge.

Change is difficult for autistic people and it needs advance planning, preparation and structure for it to be successful. Transition from college to work should essentially follow a similar pattern as from school to college, but the following should also be taken into account:

- Transition takes time and students will need support identifying suitable types and places of work, visiting potential places of employment, filling in application forms and attending interviews.

- Potential employers will need to be made aware of the needs of the autistic person and initially supported in employing them.

- On the job training will need to be given to employers and prospective colleagues so that they can continue to work effectively with the autistic student.

- A familiar person, who is skilled in ASC employment support, should accompany the student for the period of transition.

- A person who is skilled in the areas of ASC employment support should be identified to provide continued regular support to the employer and employee, after the period of transition.

In practice, transition from college to work is more difficult to provide than from school to college because of the organizational constraints which college impose. This can be easier to negotiate if funding had been provided for extra curricula teaching in the area of 'life skills'. This enables the development of work-related skills to be taught, which can lead to work experience placements with the accompanying support. Transition to work is also easier to effectively coordinate if the student is studying a vocational course which includes a work placement. This allows for college staff to support the student in the workplace, and can form the basis of a transition to work programme. Difficulties are more likely to arise when students are studying academic courses and leave college without either of these structures in place. This should be anticipated and support from outside of the college should be sought and set up in advance. This can be a bit of a lottery, depending on where you live. Some areas have access to ASC-specific work support schemes such as Prospects or The Integrated Resource (in Sheffield), and some parent support groups have set up similar schemes, as in Norfolk, but many areas have no provision for employment support. In these situations, all autistic students entering the world of employment should request an access to work assessment from their local Job Centre Plus. This should identify the nature of the support that is needed and also provide support for them and their employers.

Experience suggests that the key to successful transition to university is to provide as much advance information and clear guidelines for support as is possible. Universities generally do not have ASC specialists and consequently have little experience, knowledge and skills of supporting autistic students. They need considerable guidance but are generally willing to learn and things are slowly improving.

2. Admissions and exclusions policies

In Chapter 1, I discussed how inflexible organizational procedures and practices can present barriers for autistic students. Reasonable adjustments should therefore be made to remove the disadvantage caused by these. It is not acceptable for a college to refuse to admit or enrol any student because they have a disability and all admissions procedures should reflect this. Unfortunately, 'hidden disabilities' are rarely accommodated in this area. There are a number of ways in which reasonable adjustments can be made:

- If the autistic student experiences difficulty in handwriting, then they should be allowed to type their application form or have someone else to write it for them.

- If the autistic person has difficulty communicating their thoughts in the written word, then information which is presented in an alternative media should be considered as a supplement to their application form. This could be an audio or visual recording which allows them to address the application form orally, or a video recording which demonstrates their ability and skills in the relevant area.

- Interviews are extremely stressful for all interviewees, but the autistic person is at a substantial disadvantage to other students because of their disability. Reasonable adjustments should be made which include ensuring a 'low arousal' environment, and which give the student the opportunity to view the location and meet the interviewers in advance. The format and structure of the interview should also be given in advance to minimize stress. Extra time should be allowed if needed to accommodate any differences which the autistic person experiences in information processing. The autistic person should be allowed to have support at interview and the interviewers should include someone with ASC specialist skills present. Conditions of acceptance should not be made which do not apply to other students.

- It is reasonable to expect that all staff who work with autistic students should have a full understanding of what inclusion means in relation to autism. Staff should also be given training which provides guidelines on inclusive practices in the area of 'hidden disabilities' including autism. This should also be reflected in the development and implementation of bullying policies. Far too often, autistic students are excluded from school because of their inappropriate behaviour which has in fact been in response to the bullying which they have been subjected to. The term 'brought it on themselves', should never be applied in cases of bullying, but is frequently used in schools and colleges. ASC training should minimize this.

3. Timetabling

Timetables can be reasonably adjusted to accommodate the needs of autistic students. The key to this is flexibility and a willingness to 'mix and match'. College life is extremely hard work for autistic people who have to employ significant amounts of extra energy in information processing and 'pretending to be normal'. Autistic 'fascinations' may also mean that there is a certain time during the week when it is not possible for them to be in college. Occasionally, an urgent need for social skills teaching may have to take precedence over academic subject teaching. The result is that autistic students may not always be able to complete a full day's or a full week's timetable. Solutions can often be found which extend the length of the course for the autistic student or enable them to join a different group for one subject. Alternatively, it may only be possible for an autistic student to follow a limited number of modules at a time. This should be allowed and the student may be able to complete the other modules at a later date. If necessary, a student should be given a 'tailor made' timetable.

4. Staff training

This has already been discussed and in itself is a reasonable adjustment. Without it, staff are unable to make reasonable adjustments to their own practice or be aware of which adjustments they should recommend for their students.

5. Specialist support

The arguments for this have already been provided in earlier chapters. In itself, it constitutes a reasonable adjustment.

6. Outings and trips

Autistic students are often excluded from outings and trips because they cannot be supported. This should not happen and specialist support should always be provided to suit their needs. There are occasions however, when compulsory attendance on outings or visits can present very real problems for autistic students who find unpredictability and change too challenging and difficult to cope with. Reasonable adjustments would be to provide extra preparation time for the visit, using ASC specialist tools such as Social Stories™. Alternatively, if it is too distressing for the student to participate, it would be appropriate to seek alternative solutions such as videoing the visit and working through it with the student. Both constitute 'reasonable adjustments' and do not compromise academic standards.

7. Equipment and resources

Differences in information processing, thinking and communicating, as well as TOM impact significantly on an autistic student's learning. These can be accommodated by allowing the use of the following in both the delivery and assessment of the curriculum:

- IT
- video recording
- audio recording
- speed text typist
- ASC-specific note takers
- ASC-differentiated materials.

If it is thought that the first three of these will advantage an autistic student over their non-autistic peers in terms of their assessment, then these options can easily be extended to include them also.

8. Work placement provision

I have unfortunately experienced two instances, both involving bakery courses, when students were excluded from work placements.

Excuses were made relating to health and safety issues but the under-lying reasons in both instances were prejudice and discrimination. If an autistic student has been accepted onto a course of which a work placement is a part, then it is not acceptable for them to be excluded because of their disability and the prejudice and discrimination which underpins such exclusions should always be challenged. Of course it would not be good practice to place any students in a position where their health and safety or that of others might be at risk because of their disability, but an accurate assessment of this must be made by ASC and subject specialists first. Most safety risks are removed when support is provided and it is reasonable to provide this in the workplace for autistic students. The nature of autism probably also requires that the student be supported so this is not an additional requirement. It is also reasonable to 'hand pick' a placement to suit the student's needs and to provide extra preparation, visits and plan-ning time. Workplace supervisors should also be visited and briefed (with the student's permission) on the nature of the student's disability.

9. Specialist advice services

Colleges vary in the types of advice services which they offer to all stu-dents, but most offer counselling and 'welfare advice'. Without ASC knowledge and skills, these can be quite problematic for autistic stu-dents. Counsellors should always receive additional training in autism awareness and autism thinking, learning and behaviour of the type described in Chapter 5. Without this understanding, misunderstand-ings can be made which have potentially damaging implications, so advisors should also work closely with ASC specialists. It is sometimes claimed that the nature of the relationship requires confidentiality, and as a result cannot involve other people. As already discussed in Chapter 4, the nature of confidentiality can be misunderstood and taken to mean secrecy, when in fact it means ensuring that information is acces-sible only to those who are authorized to have access to it. Assumptions should not be made that the autistic person would not want to be sup-ported in these situations and they should be given the opportunity to choose this if so desired. It is also possible to discuss an individual's autism in a general way without disclosing confidences.

10. Teaching methods and practices

Braille and BSL translators constitute reasonable adjustments for blind and deaf students. In the same way, ASC-specific communication and materials provide reasonable adjustments for autistic students. It is therefore reasonable to make some adjustments to our teaching methods and practices.

'Autism specific' is often inaccurately used to mean 'taking autism into consideration' when in fact it involves much more than that. 'Autism specific' means using our general knowledge of autism, which we have gained from our experience of working with autistic people, together with our study of the theories and personal accounts of autism, and then combining these with our knowledge of the individual student and applying it to our practice. In terms of making reasonable adjustments it should impact on our classroom management, communication skills and choice of materials, as well as our methods of assessing and teaching. This is not as daunting as it may sound as most good teachers already utilize many ASC-specific skills. In addition, ASC-specific methods have a positive effect on the whole class and minimize the behavioural difficulties which may be experienced from others. The following are only suggestions for adjustments, based on what I have found to be useful in some instances. I have included them to give ideas and to encourage you to be creative in your approach, but it is important to remember that not all of these work for all autistic people.

CLASSROOM MANAGEMENT

- Organize the seating to minimize distractions.
- Place displays at the back of the room to avoid distractions.
- Utilize screens to make private spaces if necessary.
- Structure lessons and give a visible plan.
- Avoid noisy activities or provide 'time out'.

- Encourage a quiet learning environment.

- Use soft music as background noise.

- Control lighting using coloured tissue paper if necessary.

- Provide a seating plan and ensure that students stick to it.

COMMUNICATION SKILLS

- Give extra time to process information.

- Use a quiet, calm, even voice.

- Use clear and concise language and avoid superfluous information.

- Avoid or explain euphemisms and figures of speech.

- Avoid touching.

- Provide visual instructions.

- Supplement spoken communication with visual media.

- Explain abstract concepts.

- Provide memory aids.

- Be aware that perfume and scented toiletries may cause sensory over-stimulation, as can the eating of strong flavoured foods and the wearing of bright colours and some fabric textures.

CHOICE OF MATERIALS

Materials should be differentiated to make them autism specific. Differentiation has become synonymous with simplification and this is not the correct use or understanding of the term. Differentiation is to do with recognizing and addressing differences. In terms of education, differentiation recognizes and addresses different ways of learning. In terms of autism, differentiation of materials means making them 'autism specific' as described above. This can be done by:

- making them as visual and as structured as possible

- avoiding and removing ambiguities in language

- removing any information which is superfluous to the task

- breaking down tasks

- making abstract concepts concrete

- avoiding materials which might cause sensory overload

- providing clear indicators of how to start and finish

- modifying individual tasks.

EXAMINATIONS

All forms of assessment ought to be adjusted so that autistic students are not disadvantaged and differentiation should apply to assessment in the same way as it does to teaching materials. In this way the deficits or impairments which are associated with autism can be accommodated. Course work and internal assessments are easily differentiated but there is less control over external exams. The Integrated Resource website records that examination boards are kind to them and award their students many concessions, including the use of a translator to compensate for impairments in the semantic and pragmatic aspects of autism. My experience has been that despite many requests for a translator and challenges to their decisions, examination boards have only allowed the following concessions:

- 25 per cent extra time

- a reader and then only if the student's reading age is significantly below their chronological age

- a scribe or the use of a computer (if there is supporting evidence that handwriting is significantly impaired)

- a prompt (to move students on to the next question)

- breaks

- a separate room.

It is my view that concessions should apply across the board and to not do so is discriminatory. Professionals and parents should continue to challenge the exam boards on the issue of translation.

TEACHING METHODS

Generally, visual and kinaesthetic teaching methods work best for autistic students. This does not mean that no auditory methods should be used as these may be the preferred learning style of other class members. Differentiation through teaching methods is best utilized by giving a choice of methods for individual tasks. Useful tools for this are:

- mind maps

- video

- role-play

- simulations

- flow charts

- diagrams and pictures

- games, puzzles, true or false exercises etc.

- Social Stories™, social scripts, storyboards and cartoons.

The key to using the most suitable teaching methods is getting to know and understand your student. Work with their 'fascinations' rather than against them and use them as ways of developing interests and skills. Don't assume prior knowledge or skills in any area and teach appropriate classroom behaviour, organizational skills and cause and effect. Manage behaviour by utilizing the following:

- Recognize behaviour as a form of communication.

- Check for emotional or sensory overload and reduce or remove the stimuli.

- Avoid direct confrontation and arguments.

- Reduce anxiety by providing structure and choice.

- Reduce incoming information.

- Be flexible and willing to back off.

- Provide frequent breaks and time out.

- Allow time for 'fascinations' and teach and encourage the use of socially appropriate coping strategies.

- Be creative and inventive in your approach and always check for understanding.

- Reflect on your practice and ask yourself the following questions:

  ◦ Am I using too many words?

  ◦ Am I speaking too loudly?

  ◦ Am I too directly confrontational? (e.g. forcing eye contact).

  ◦ Am I causing confusion?

  ◦ Am I causing sensory overload?

  ◦ Have I provided visual information?

  ◦ Is my language clear, abstract or ambiguous?

  ◦ Am I explaining abstract concepts such as time?

  ◦ How can I develop more autism friendly communication?

One word of caution! Recognize that you are part of the environment and that you may be contributing to sensory over-stimulation. Be aware of the effect which your use of perfumes, colours and textures may have on some autistic people, and if these are problematic be prepared to change them.

It is important to recognize that the job you do is difficult and stressful. You are only human and we all make mistakes. Don't blame yourself if things don't go according to plan. Spend some time observing, discussing and reflecting on what may have gone wrong, but then move on to planning future strategies and action which will avoid their repetition.

11. The curriculum

A great deal of concern has been voiced recently on the suitability of the school curriculum for less academically able students. If this concern is applied to autistic students, then it takes on an added dimension as in many instances, the accepted curriculum is also not suitable for the more academically able autistic student. This can be extremely problematic as we have no alternative but to work within the system, whilst we challenge it to change. In many ways, this can be far less problematic in FE than it is in school, partly because FE students (if they have been guided and advised correctly), have already chosen to study areas which are more suited to their interests, skills and ability. There is also more flexibility in FE and students are able to study in a less prescriptive and more 'modular' way. This encourages and enables more choice and flexibility. However, it would be wrong to give the impression that the FE curriculum is totally suitable for autistic students. This is rarely the case and adjustments have to be made. In some instances, it is not possible to make adjustments without compromising the academic standards of the course, and it is clearly not reasonable to do this. When this is the case, then acceptable adjustments should be made and the student will need to be counselled to understand the implications of the restrictions for them and their grade.

There is no reason why an autistic student cannot follow an individual curriculum which is tailored to their need. It is unconventional, but not unreasonable, to enable students to pick and match from a variety of options from different courses. Some courses, particularly at a basic level are designed around this type of framework. When this is the case, then the autistic student can slot into the existing provision. There will be problems of certification, if students pick and mix without completing full courses, but this raises issues which challenge the ethos and organization of education and learning in a way which is beyond the remit of this book. These issues should however, be challenged at every opportunity.

In the current system, students who study academic courses have no option but to conform to the requirements of the course. When this is the case, adjustments should be made to the curriculum in the form of differentiated teaching and assessment as described above. This can make an apparently inaccessible curriculum much more accessible for the autistic student. It is also reasonable for the autistic student to be given technical tutorials to assist in areas of the curriculum that are particularly difficult for them. On occasions, the qualification has more significance for the student than the education and at these times, we have to teach the autistic student how to 'jump through the hoops' to enable them to 'play the game' in the same way as their neuro-typical peers. This may present ethical dilemmas for some people, but the reality is that most of us are quite skilled in this particular area, whilst the autistic person is not. 'Jumping through hoops' and 'playing the game' are social skills and for the autistic person, will require specific teaching. The teaching of social skills to autistic people is in itself a reasonable adjustment to the curriculum. This is discussed in the next chapter.

CHAPTER 7

The 'Hidden Curriculum'

It is widely recognized and accepted that autistic people do not learn social behaviour in the same way as their neuro-typical peers. The reasons for this become very apparent, when we understand the theories discussed in the previous chapter.

Briefly, Donna Williams (1996) suggests that autistic people experience problems in accessing, processing and monitoring incoming information and that this results in them also experiencing problems in the areas of tolerance and control; this view is compatible with Central Coherence Theory, which also suggests that autistic people process information differently, focusing on the details of the social situation, at the expense of the whole. The Triad of Impairments identifies that autistic people have impairments in the areas of communication, interaction and imagination, whilst Theory of Mind suggests that autistic people lack the ability to understand mental states. Effective social and life skills require all of these things, so it is inevitable that their acquisition is significantly affected by autism. Together, social and life skills make up the 'hidden curriculum' for autistic people.

Social skills

There appears to be very little consensus as to what social skills are as can be seen from the following quotation: 'Everyone seems to know what good and bad social skills are but no one can define them adequately' (Curran and Monti 1982). Perhaps this is why the area of social skills is fraught with difficulty.

When I deliver training to practitioners on this area of work, it quickly becomes evident that there is something uncomfortable about the area of social skills, because it refers to 'social norms'. Social norms are shared customs, beliefs and behaviours which are adopted by any given society at any point in time. They are the dominant values of society which are culturally constructed and to a certain extent negotiable. They vary from culture to culture and from one historical period to another. They are essentially to do with what is acceptable in terms of behaviour, values, attitudes and beliefs. Currently, there is assumed to be a level of tolerance in Western society which allows for comparatively broad and flexible boundaries to social norms, which are continually being renegotiated in some areas. Tolerance is however, only extended within certain limits, and behaviour which strays too far beyond the tolerable limits is judged as 'inappropriate', 'deviant' or 'perverted'. Social norms are therefore inextricably linked to conformity, with the dominant members in a society requiring conformity to their views. Autism does not conform to the dominant view and autistic people are often seen as society's misfits, being labelled as 'eccentric', or as Luke Jackson has pointed out 'freaky' or 'geeky'. In the worst instances, autistic people are described as 'deviants' or 'perverts'.

Matson and Ollendick (1988) define social skills as 'a person's ability to get on with others and to engage in pro-social behaviour' (p.124). They suggest that social skills are the tools which enable a person to get on with their peers and other people who they come into contact with, and determine a person's popularity. Whilst this definition may be useful in describing the effects of social skills on a person's experience, it still does not give a clear understanding or examples of what a 'social skill' might be. A more accurate definition might be that the term 'social skills' refers to an unwritten code of acceptable behaviour, which the majority of people in a particular society are aware of, and comply with, achieving various degrees of success. This identifies that 'social skills' are not overt rules, but are 'unwritten' and covert; they are not something which we either have or don't have but are something which we can develop competence in. This challenges the view of the autistic person as 'lacking social skills' and suggests that the autistic person can improve on their competence level.

The covert and 'unwritten' nature of social skills impacts on how a person acquires them. Skills are taught and learnt and this is true of social skills, but the 'unwritten' and covert nature of social skills affects and is affected by the process in which they are acquired. It is generally thought that social skills are learnt through the 'teaching' process of socialization. Autistic people are challenged by this process of learning as their thinking and learning styles do not enable them to readily 'pick up' information in the way which socialization requires. Because of this, autistic people require social skills to be taught in a different and specific way, a way which can be accessed, processed and monitored by them.

The dilemma

People react differently to the idea of teaching social skills and there is a very real ethical and moral dilemma which I think must be faced before embarking on such a programme of teaching. The dilemma hinges on the value judgement which has to be made in determining what is 'acceptable' in another person's behaviour, and whether another individual has the right to make such a judgement about someone else, particularly when that someone is not their child. This is less of an issue in schools where the boundaries of the adult–child relationship allow for a certain involvement at this level, but becomes more significant when the students are adults. This is further affected by the issues of personal choice and rights. The ethos of FE gives a level of control to students for their own learning and actions. With this control comes responsibility and assumptions are made that students, if they are treated as adults and are given some control, then they will also assume some responsibility for their actions. This works for some students, but there are many, who at the age of 16 are not yet able to deal with this level of responsibility and 'opt out' in a variety of ways. When this happens, the concept of 'personal choice' is evoked. This usually takes the form of 'It's their choice whether to attend or not' or 'I have talked to them about it and it is their choice to …'. This is similarly voiced regarding the notion of 'rights' as in 'they have a right to refuse support' or 'they have a right to wear what they want', but of course other people also have rights and autistic people also have to 'accept the consequences' for their actions. When the notions of 'personal choice', 'rights', 'responsibility' and 'control' are applied to autistic students, without a full understanding of their condition, then the situation becomes problematic. Of course the autistic person has a right to all of these things and they also have the fundamental human right to be autistic, but as I have described in the previous chapter, the thing which we call 'autism' is not the behaviour which we observe to diagnose the condition, but is an internal reality. The problems occur when we mistakenly apply the notions of 'personal choice', 'rights', 'responsibility' and 'control' to the symptoms of autism, that is, the behaviour. This is the root of what for some people is both a moral and ethical dilemma.

Extreme examples of behaviour present no dilemmas. For example, damaging people and property is clearly unacceptable behaviour and it is considered appropriate to reprimand and correct it. Less extreme examples such as being rude to people, dominating conversations, or boring people are more subjective and present much more of a dilemma, especially when working with an older age group. The dilemma becomes even more pronounced when considering such things as choice of clothes or personal habits. Working with autistic people extends the role of 'teacher' into some very personal areas, which we would never consider appropriate with most other students, and practitioners should be clear as to where they stand in terms of what they consider to be morally and ethically appropriate. Before embarking on teaching social skills, we must therefore ask ourselves the questions: do we have the right to decide what behaviour is appropriate in these areas? And: do we have the right to teach other people how to behave? As I have said, these issues often sit uncomfortably within the FE ethos and perhaps with our own personal moral and ethical codes.

This dilemma has to be faced on an individual and personal level and I think that there are no right and wrong answers or ways to resolve it. For some people the dilemma is greater than for others, but it is essential that the dilemma is recognized, confronted and resolved, if individuals are to be effective in teaching social skills. Experience suggests that there will be negative responses and criticism to such teaching, from colleagues who lack awareness of the issues which autistic people face in this area and who feel that teaching social skills patronizes students and takes away their dignity and rights. Negativity and criticism can be difficult to deal with if there is any personal uncertainty or insecurity and anyone who embarks on teaching social skills to autistic people must be certain in their own minds of the appropriateness of the task. Without this certainty, social skills teaching will be adversely affected and consequently less effective. If you have any doubts regarding the ethical and moral issues of teaching social skills, then I would advise that you leave this area of teaching to someone who does not. However, you will probably recognize that it is virtually impossible to work with autistic people without addressing the area of social skills in some way.

I personally found the teaching of social skills a huge dilemma because I was brought up not to be a follower, and to question the status quo. Intellectually, I do not like the concept of conformity, preferring one of individuality, so teaching people to 'fit in' does not sit easily with me. Because of this, I agonized over whether teaching anyone how to 'fit in', which is essentially what teaching social skills is, was appropriate for me and them. Autistic people really challenged my views, and taught me that it is possible to teach social skills whilst maintaining the individual's right to their individuality and to their autism.

It is naïve and irresponsible to think that choices and decisions should be given to people based purely on their chronological age, without first of all ensuring that they have the knowledge and experience to guide them in making those decisions. If we apply the concepts of 'personal choice', 'rights', 'responsibility' and 'control' to autism as defined by the 'symptoms' then this is precisely what we are doing. If however, we define autism as the reality which the autistic person experiences, and then apply these concepts, the situation becomes quite different. If we then listen to what autistic people tell us, they make it clear that it is right to teach them social skills. They also make it clear to us which social skills we should teach and the level of competence to which we should teach them.

Lack of, or limited competence in the area of social skills is a 'typical' feature of autism which leads to prejudice and discrimination and as such presents as a barrier which disables autistic people. Solutions therefore should be sought and applied to the removal of this barrier. If we view the barrier as having or possessing a 'lack of social skills', we automatically locate the 'problem' within the autistic person. If however, we view the barrier in terms of acquiring a level of skill or competence in the area of social skills, then we shift the focus to one of teaching and are better able to identify the societal barriers which hinder learning. As has already been mentioned, it is generally accepted that social skills are acquired through the process of socialization. This process or method of teaching is not effective for autistic people due to the 'difference' between autistic and neuro-typical thinking, which is outlined in the beginning of the previous chapter, and in itself presents a barrier to the learning of social skills. To remove this barrier requires alternative methods of teaching. If we do not provide alternative methods of teaching social skills, then we are inadvertently perpetuating the prejudice and discrimination which autistic people experience. This is not to suggest that we force the teaching of social skills onto autistic people, but we do have a responsibility to ensure that they have the knowledge and experience which enables them to make the 'personal choices', assert their 'rights' and take 'responsibility' and 'control' for their actions and behaviour, to a similar degree as their neuro-typical peers. Social skills are the tools which enable this. I believe that if we do not teach competence in this area, then we fail in our responsibility towards autistic people.

How to teach social skills

I have assumed that all FE colleges endorse the teaching of the 'hidden curriculum' which is associated with autism. I do recognize that this is not always the case and that some colleges will take the view that the teaching of any social or life skills is beyond their educational remit and should be the responsibility of students' parents. When this is the case, the argument should be put forward that the teaching of social skills is a reasonable adjustment which addresses the disadvantage which autistic students experience, when compared with their neuro-typical peers. The educational curriculum requires a certain level of competence in many areas of social skill and without specific teaching in this area autistic students are denied full access to the curriculum. I have sometimes been told that there are issues of funding. My experience has been that if the teaching of 'life skills' or 'social skills' is presented as part of the autistic student's learning 'package', then there is no difficulty in negotiating the relevant funding.

The difficulties in 'making connections', or processing incoming information, which autistic people experience, often results in difficulties with recognizing the significance of acquired knowledge, for other social situations. Knowledge gained in one social situation is therefore often not applied or transferred by the autistic person to other similar situations. Because of this, it is well recognized that social skills are best taught and acquired in real life contexts. This does not however, mean that all social skills teaching should take place outside of the college environment. On the contrary, most social skills teaching will take place in the college, but at different levels.

- The first level is integral to the student's support. If the student receives ASC specialist support, the support workers, whether they are lecturers or learner support assistants will be trained, and engaged on a daily basis, in teaching social skills as part of the student's support package. In addition, if the training guidelines which are given in Chapter 5 have been followed, then all staff who have contact with autistic students will have received training which enables them to sensitively teach appropriate social skills, in all settings.

- The second level is required for specific skills which need formal teaching as preparation before taking into real life. This teaching should take place out of context, in a one-to-one setting with an ASC specialist who has been trained in teaching social skills.

- The third level takes place in context and is concerned with transferring the skills learnt and practised at level 2, to the real world situation. This might be outside college.

I am often asked my opinion on teaching social skills in small groups. This idea is often put forward because of funding issues concerning one-to-one teaching. When this is the case, my view is that funding needs should never be put before the individual needs of students, and the nature of autism is such that individual solutions need to be found for the individual barriers which autistic people face. This requires one-to-one teaching. The second reason, which is the one which is usually given for suggesting this, is that group interaction aids learning. It is my experience that the development of social skills is aided by group interaction, but only by inclusive group interaction. That is, when autistic students interact, with support, in small groups with their neuro-typical peers. I have found teaching social skills in 'discrete' autism or 'learning disabled' groups, to rarely work unless the teaching of skills is mechanical and non-transferable. I have also found that it is essential for teaching in this area to be person-centred and student-led and as individual student's needs differ enormously, this tends to be impractical to address in group situations. I believe that there is sometimes a place for discrete group teaching and this is between the second and third stages suggested above. This would provide opportunity for autistic students to practice the skills they have learnt in the classroom in a small group situation. This however, presupposes that there will be a group of autistic students who are all in a position to practise these at the same time and this is rarely the case. During most of my time in FE, I fought for one-to-one social skills teaching and resisted the discrete groups, because of this.

Without relevance and purpose, social skills teaching is little more than 'obedience training' which is dehumanizing, mechanical and has limited effect. It is also not in keeping with a person-centred approach which is advocated throughout this book. A person-centred approach makes the autistic person the focus for all planning, for a provision which is developed around them. This ensures the appropriateness and relevance of teaching social skills, which will have been identified as part of the profiling process suggested in Chapter 2. The involvement of the autistic person in this process also enables the development of a sense of purpose and provides motivation. As well as identifying the areas of social skill which it is appropriate to teach, the profiling process will identify the level at which to teach it.

Level 1 teaching

Often, practitioners who are described as supporters rather than teachers tell me that they are not involved in delivering social skills teaching. When I ask how students are supported in managing their behaviour however, they are quite clear of their involvement. I understand that role and salary differentials leads to the need for clear boundaries which reflect the responsibilities which are attached to those roles and salaries, but I do think that this has, in some instances been over-applied to our language use. Whether we use the words 'assist', 'support' or 'train' to describe what support workers do, at the end of the day, teaching social skills is an unavoidable part of their role. Simply explaining to someone for example, that looking out of the window when someone is talking to them results in the other person thinking that they are not listening, is teaching a social skill. Support workers do this sort of thing on a daily basis.

With regard to behaviour, support workers tell me that they:

- correct students' inappropriate behaviours

- encourage students' appropriate behaviour

- explain why some behaviour is inappropriate

- provide students with strategies for managing their own behaviour

- support students in developing new behaviours and skills.

The danger in not recognizing this as teaching social skills is that it becomes subject to individual fancy, with the result that it can be inconsistent, confusing and conflicting. There is also a danger that individuals may impose their own moral and ethical values on the student. In most cases, this may not be a problem, but there are instances where personal values can clash with family values or those of the dominant culture. This is particularly evident in areas such as religion, social class and politics. Safeguards must be in place to define the boundaries and ensure that this does not happen.

Through experience, I have learnt that safeguards can be set and these types of problems avoided by following the four stages of profiling which are described in Chapter 2:

1. Gather information.

2. Assess the information.

3. Make recommendations (which are implemented).

4. Evaluate and reassess.

The process suggested ensures that other people are involved throughout, and provides a forum for the discussion and identification of possible personal bias. It also provides a framework for accountability and enables a level of 'competence' to be defined which is applicable for the individual student. Information is gathered through observation and discussion with others (including the student). It is then analysed in discussion with others and recommendations for teaching made from this. In this way, the autistic student has ownership of the skill which is to be taught which ensures relevance and encourages motivation.

Example 1: Charlie

Charlie has a diagnosis of high functioning autism. His profile has already identified some areas of social skills teaching, but further observations are that he gulps air, breaks wind, shouts out and squeals loudly during lessons. None of Charlie's peers will sit next to him as a result and his subject lecturers are finding his behaviour disruptive. There is also a suggestion that Charlie is being called names during unsupervised times. In the profile evaluation discussions which take place involving Charlie, his support workers and his parents, Charlie states that he is unhappy sitting on his own. The reasons for this are 'discussed' with Charlie using ASC-specific methods, and Charlie, with the support of his parents decides that he would like to try to manage this behaviour. Strategies are put in place which involve managing Charlie's diet, suggesting that he sucks a sweet to help him to manage his gulping, and negotiating extra toilet breaks. Charlie agrees to write his favourite words which he shouts out, on cards which are laminated and placed on his desk. Instead of shouting them in lessons, he is encouraged to pick them up and show them to his support worker. Despite their individual views, all Charlie's support workers agree that if he is breaking wind, they will suggest that he goes to the toilet. They also agree to consistently provide Charlie with a sweet to help him gulp less air and agree to use the same phrase to assist Charlie in managing his shouting and squealing. Charlie is also given opportunities for 'time out' to help reduce his stress levels. Charlie's parents agree to use the same strategies at home.

It is also agreed that Charlie's peer group should receive autism awareness training to enable them to be more understanding of his behaviour and to encourage them to assist him.

A period of one month is set for evaluation and assessment, which follows the same procedure as already described.

The evaluation indicates that the change of diet and other strategies have significantly minimized Charlie's digestive difficulties. He continues to gulp air, although the instances are reduced. The group discussion results in the opinion that Charlie has reached a level of sufficient competency in these areas and his peers are initiating some reconciliation as a result of this and their awareness training. The strategies employed in reducing Charlie's spontaneous shouting and squealing however, have had limited success. 'Discussions' with Charlie suggest that it is appropriate to identify and implement further strategies at this stage.

There will of course be times when support workers have to spontaneously 'teach' social skills without initiating the above process. The previous use of the process and good communication between all team members will however, contribute significantly towards ensuring that in these instances, moral and ethical boundaries are adhered to.

Level 2 teaching

This level of teaching is not always necessary or appropriate for all autistic students and should be guided by the profiling process, which should be applied in the same way as to level 1 teaching. Level 2 teaching takes place in a more formal way. Both levels of teaching require 'autism-specific' teaching and skills, and these are crucial at this level. I would recommend that level 2 teaching should only be considered by ASC specialists who have received training in the area of teaching social skills. In Chapter 6, I described 'autism specific' as meaning 'using our general knowledge of autism, which we have gained from our experience of working with autistic people, together with our study of the theories and personal accounts of autism, and then combining these with our knowledge of the individual student and applying it to our practice'. By this definition, being 'autism specific' guides our practice and influences decisions about all aspects of teaching at this level. As well as indicating if and when it is appropriate to teach social skills (the why to teach), being autism specific also guides the choice of:

- where to teach
- what to teach
- how to teach
- when to teach.

I realize that for a lot of people, the individual nature of autism can appear to require levels of input which seem daunting or even impossible. Because of this, I am often asked to recommend an 'off the peg' programme of social skills teaching which can be used for groups of autistic students and people are disappointed when I fail to provide this. 'Autism specific' and 'person centred' are fundamental aspects of good practice in this field. Both are incompatible with 'off the peg' group teaching and like most skills, both get quicker and easier with practice. I have known instances where practitioners have used 'off the peg' social skills packages which have been designed for students who have general learning difficulties, and in some instances, I have known people to claim that these have been 'successful'. This has not been my experience, however.

My experience suggests that the main factors in successful social skills teaching are that it should be:

1. person centred

2. autism specific

3. relevant

4. well planned

5. well structured

6. flexible.

The need for flexibility may appear to contradict some of the other factors suggested, but it is essential to ensure relevance. Sometimes, the autistic student will bring more pressing needs to the social skills teaching session with them. When this happens, it is essential that there is enough flexibility to abort the planned lesson and address the more urgent matter. In such instances there is no alternative but to 'ad lib'. This of course should be in an 'autism-specific' way!

The need for self-awareness

There will be differing levels of self-awareness amongst the autistic students who access FE. This will range from those who have no idea that they are autistic, but perhaps recognize that they are a bit 'different' from everyone else, to those who have known that they are autistic from a young age and who have a sophisticated understanding of what that means for them. Social skills teaching presupposes that the student recognizes the need for being taught and takes the student's autism as its starting point. Recognizing the need for such teaching involves the autistic student recognizing that they are different from their peers who do not need to be taught social skills in a formal way. In some instances, therefore, social skills teaching first of all requires teaching the autistic person that they have autism and how this affects them. This is of course something which should not be done in isolation from other aspects of the student's life and will require the permission and cooperation of the student's parents. The profiling process will have already provided a useful vehicle for such issues to be raised and will also have identified the appropriateness of social skills teaching. In instances when students are not aware of their autism, then autism self-awareness teaching should be provided.

In *Access and Inclusion for Children with Autistic Spectrum Disorders* (Hesmondhalgh and Breakey 2001), I described autism awareness teaching under the title of 'Counselling'. This used the Triad of Impairments as its starting point for enabling the autistic student to understand the nature of their condition. As my knowledge and understanding of autism has developed, I have changed my approach in this area to make it more 'autism specific', 'person centred' and more in line with the social model of disability. This has involved subtle changes as follows:

1. I now include an ability to work in an autism-specific way as an essential prerequisite for all practitioners who embark on teaching an autism self-awareness programme.

2. I no longer see the study of the psychology of 'the self' as a prerequisite to teaching, preferring to suggest that practitioners are well read in autistic people's explanations of this concept.

3. I no longer use the Triad of Impairments as the starting point in the explanations of autism, preferring to start with Donna Williams' explanation which I have outlined in Chapter 6.

4. I also now include Central Coherence Theory in my teaching.

5. In the personal management of autism I also focus on how other people's attitudes and practices can be changed to provide adjustments for autistic students.

6. I also teach self-advocacy skills which assist the autistic person in disclosing their condition to others and negotiating 'reasonable adjustments'.

The fundamental process for autism awareness teaching is still however relatively unchanged and I would refer the reader to the original chapter as referenced above. I would emphasize the importance of ensuring that practitioners who undertake this type of teaching have no hidden negative attitudes towards autism as these can be passed on to the autistic student. It is also important to emphasize that this sort of teaching can not be entered into lightly. It is hugely challenging for the autistic person and there will be painful issues which need to be handled with sensitivity and care. In my experience, an awareness of one's autism is essential to the learning of social skills because the learning and consequently the teaching has to come from the perspective of the autistic person. A knowledge of 'self' is required for this

Which skills to teach?

It takes time to change people's mind set, and people often ask me what areas of social skills should be taught. Again, from an 'autism-specific', person-centred perspective, it is impossible to be prescriptive as you must teach what is required by the individual student at that particular time. I have however, taught social skills in the following areas:

- all aspects of non-verbal behaviour

- managing pitch and tone of voice

- the appropriateness and inappropriateness of swearing

- what constitutes 'rude'

- making friends

- managing fascinations

- managing boredom

- understanding emotions

- personal appearance

- intimate relationships

- understanding other people's behaviour.

The main guidelines, based on ten years' experience in this area, which I would give to anyone involved in delivering social skills teaching are:

1. Plan thoroughly. This starts with getting to know the student you are working with. Participation in the profiling should have identified communication preferences and strengths as well as thinking and learning styles.

2. Utilize all the autism-specific skills which are identified in Chapter 6 as 'reasonable adjustments' to teaching methods.

3. Be explicit. This is particularly important because the sensitive nature of the task often causes embarrassment for the non-autistic practitioner. This results in skirting around the topic or implying meaning which it is assumed is shared by the autistic person, when it is not. There is no way out of this. Autistic students will miss the point if you are not clear, direct and explicit in both your use of language and choice of materials. Check for any specific vocabulary which you should use.

4. Be sensitive to the autistic student's responses and provide means of checking how they are feeling. Drawings of faces can provide a good checklist for this. I personally prefer to ask the autistic person to draw their own faces for the different emotions as this gives a clearer indication of what they associate with that emotion, but Tony Attwood (1998, p.194) provides good drawings which can be used for this purpose.

5. Give the student a means of indicating if they need to stop. This can be any sign which is previously agreed between you both. I have used red and yellow cards with one student who was a keen football supporter. Showing me the yellow card indicated that he was beginning to feel uncomfortable, so I knew to proceed with caution and the red card indicated that I should stop, without question. Another student chose to bang the table once.

6. Involve parents and carers at every stage as there might be repercussions at home. I usually communicate immediately with parents and carers, and set homework which enables the autistic person to put into practice what has been taught during the session. This encourages the 'parents as partners' approach.

7. Use visual forms of communication such as social cartoons and comic strip conversations (Gray 1994). I also find flow charts, spider diagrams and drawings work well. In my experience, many autistic people enjoy role plays. These can be video recorded and studied together to improve competence. They also provide a visual record for the autistic person to measure their progress.

8. Be creative in your approach. Autism challenges us to think 'outside of the box' and that in itself is very creative. No one has the monopoly on working with autistic people. If you have an idea that something might work, first of all check out that it fits with your understanding of autism and the individual. Then, talk about it with someone else who understands the person well and if they also think it might work, try it and evaluate it. If it doesn't work, you do not have to use it again.

Example 2 on the following page arose out of desperate circumstances. I include it here because it is an example of how creativity can work.

The notion of competence

The idea that autistic people do not have social skills can be misleading. I prefer the use of the term 'social competence' as I think that it sits more comfortably with the idea of an autism spectrum. Social competence implies that there is a range of skill, which we all fit into at some point. This then suggests that there is a point where our social competency becomes 'good enough'. Perhaps, part of our profiling process should identify the point of 'good enough' to target for teaching.

Example 2: Jordan

A colleague and I had the idea for this approach independently of each other at around the same time. It initially seemed quite ridiculous, but we were trying to manage a crisis situation, so we decided to try it. We were the only two people working with this particular student so we were able to implement the approach at both level 1 and level 2 of the social skills teaching, and it worked.

Jordan is an intelligent boy whose personal account is included in Chapter 8. He experiences severe difficulties with social relationships due to autism. The difficulties he experiences with processing, accessing and monitoring incoming information lead to particular difficulties in his interpersonal relationships with his peers. Jordan is unable to read the non-verbal behaviour of his peers and also focuses on detail to the expense of 'gist' and context. As a result, he has difficulty in recognizing people if they are wearing different clothes, or telling people apart if they are wearing the same baseball cap for example. Jordan appears to be emotionally flat, and also has difficulty in identifying any emotional state in others. Jordan desires social contact, but his difficulty in processing information for meaning and relevance, has in the past led to a need for control and excessive interests in certain individuals which has destroyed any potential friendships. Jordan experiences extremely high levels of anxiety which cause emotional 'shut down' at times and has also developed a fascination with friendships. This fascination has become excessive and Jordan is very socially isolated as a result.

Jordan's desire to make friends, together with the high level of anxiety which he experiences led to the identification of the need for social skills teaching in this area. The extent of the Jordan's difficulties in the area of social skills is extremely complex, and social skills teaching is still ongoing. The following describes one way which Jordan was taught about friendships.

Jordan expected friendships to be instant and intense and this was very disconcerting for his peers. During social skills lessons, Jordan was encouraged to think of friendships as something which grow. This led to the idea of growing a garden of friendship. This lent itself quite easily to a choice of visual media and in this instance, as growing plants was impractical, drawings were chosen. Through these, Jordan was able to visualize 'seeds of friendship' which he 'planted'. He was also able to visualize that friendships 'grow' at different rates and that some do not develop past the stage of acquaintance. When Jordan was feeling anxious about a particular relationship, he was able to look at the drawings and identify the stage of the friendship. He was also able to identify strategies for nurturing the friendships, in the way that the sun and water nurture plants. This method was also used to explain how when we move on, we leave some friendships to 'die'.

The notion of competence also suggests that skills will improve with practice and this is an important aspect of social skills teaching. All level 2 type social skills should be practised and supported by level 1 type teaching. This practising in fact constitutes level 3 of social skills teaching.

Life skills

Life skills are practical skills which aid a person's independence. They are considerably less controversial than social skills, although their link with what is viewed as 'age appropriate' can present a dilemma for some people. It is widely acknowledged that autistic people have an uneven skills profile and that age and academic ability are no indicators of the level of life skills which an autistic person has acquired. For this reason, autistic people may achieve academic excellence at advanced levels, but be unable to perform what others may view as simple everyday tasks such as using public transport or managing their own personal hygiene routine. This can present problems for autistic people if they have not acquired 'age appropriate' life skills and these need to be specifically taught to them. Often, life skills teaching at college is only available to learning disabled students and the more academically able autistic students are excluded from this teaching. Colleges vary in their willingness to accommodate this hidden aspect of autism, and the opinion that this should not be a part of the academic curriculum may be valid. It is my view however, that life skills must be taught in order to fully access learning, and that quarrels over who should teach them present barriers to full inclusion for the autistic person.

Like social skills, life skills are best taught in context. This means that unlike social skills teaching, a large percentage of life skills teaching will take place outside the classroom, although there will be classroom preparation. The process and guidelines for teaching life skills are essentially the same as for teaching social skills:

- All planning and teaching should be person-centred.

- The profiling process will guide the identification of skills to teach.

- All teaching should be ASC-specific.

- All teaching should be relevant to the autistic person.

- Teaching sessions should be well planned and structured but also flexible.

As with social skills, it is not possible to be prescriptive in terms of which areas of life skills to teach, and the notion of what is 'age appropriate' will form part of the identification and planning process. I have taught life skills in the following areas:

- accessing and using public transport

- handling and managing money

- personal hygiene

- accessing and using recreational activities

- personal safety

- shopping

- dressing

- basic cooking

- using the telephone

- interview skills.

The guidelines for teaching social skills also apply to teaching life skills.

Summary

- Autistic people do not learn social behaviour in the same way as their neuro-typical peers. This leads to the need for specific teaching in the areas of social and life skills. This is often referred to as 'The Hidden Curriculum', which generally means social and life skills teaching.

- Social skills refer to an unwritten code of behaviour which society views as acceptable. This leads to an ethical and moral dilemma which practitioners should recognize and resolve before embarking on a programme of teaching social skills.

- Social skills are best taught in context, with teaching taking place on two levels. The first is integral to the nature of support, whilst the second targets specific areas for formal classroom teaching which is practised and transferred to context.

- The suggestion is made that social skills are taught best in one-to-one situations.

- Life skills refers to practical skills which aid a person's independence. These are also learnt best in context.

- The profiling process recommended in Chapter 2 guides all planning for social and life skills teaching and ensures that the teaching is person-centred and relevant.

- Guidelines are provided which ensure that all teaching methods are autism specific.

- The notion of social competence is put forward as an alternative way of viewing social skills which suggests that a 'good enough' level can be acquired.

CHAPTER 8

Individual Accounts

These three young people demonstrate in different ways what this book is about. They and others like them are the most effective teachers we will find. However much we know and however hard we might try, we will never know what it is to be autistic, but autism is their experience and their life. As well as being a success story, each of these accounts records a personal struggle. The struggle is not against autism, but is against a neuro-typical system and attitudes which exclude their neuro-diversity. The struggle for each of these autistic people is to be respected, to be listened to and to have their potential recognized and their needs met. These three accounts illustrate how in these instances this has been achieved. There is no room for complacency however, as despite their success, the struggle continues daily for all three of the people who are represented here. For each one of them, there are many more who do not experience a similar level of success.

I am very grateful to all three people and their parents for giving me permission to include their accounts in this book. It has been a privilege for me to learn from them over the years and I am immensely humbled by the confidence and trust which they have shown me. I have tried to record the experiences and opinions of each person, in the way that they and their parents told it and each account has been approved by them.

Jordan Selwood

When I asked Jordan if he would be willing for me to write about him, I offered to use a pseudonym to maintain confidentiality. Jordan's response was: 'but no one would know who I was and I would love everyone to know about me. I want them to know how well I am doing.' Jordan is quite rightly proud of his achievements.

I have chosen to include Jordan's experience in FE, because his story demonstrates how inclusion can work, even when no one expects it to. It also demonstrates the need for a 'joined up' provision of services, where everyone works in partnership to provide support for the autistic person. This was not won easily for Jordan, but has been achieved through the continued and sustained effort of his father.

Background

Jordan was born at the end of 1986, so he is 18 years old at the time of writing. He has two younger sisters and all three are cared for by their father, who has been their sole carer since late 1999. Jordan's father is unable to remember many details of Jordan's early development, partly because he was in denial at the time, but he remembers that there was some delay in meeting milestones and that Jordan was diagnosed as having autism by the age of seven, as a result. This would have been considered quite an early and unusual diagnosis at the time, in an authority which preferred to use the term 'severe communication disorder'. It would suggest that the presentation of autism was clear and undisputable in Jordan's case.

Jordan has an amazing route planning ability. He also has a phenomenal memory and remembers many of his early childhood experiences. The following account is based primarily on his recollection of events, with some confirmation from his father. I have contributed the organizational details from my records and memory of the time.

Jordan remembers starting nursery in 1989 and school in 1991. He moved school one year later, as a result of a schools' reorganization programme, to a small special needs primary school which had residential provision. It is probable, but Jordan and his father are uncertain, that the first school which Jordan attended was also in the special schools sector. This would indicate that the nature and degree of Jordan's needs was recognized from a very young age.

Jordan was very happy at primary school and remembers it with fondness. He liked the staff and felt that they understood him. The school had a family atmosphere, and Jordan was able to access the residential provision, initially for one night a week. He found this difficult at first but soon settled in and enjoyed it. This provision was increased to two nights a week during Year 6 of Jordan's time there.

Jordan finds it difficult to attribute significance to most information, but is intelligent and 'absorbs information like a sponge'. He also enjoys academic work. This ability and love of learning was influential in the decision for him to attend a mainstream secondary school in September 1998. This school had a specialist integrated resource provision for pupils with 'severe communication difficulties' and was where I first met Jordan.

Jordan initially received one-to-one ASC specialist support at The Integrated Resource Unit for 100 per cent of his time. In addition, he had specialist teaching in social and life skills. Jordan describes his time at the resource unit as being the time that he 'learnt most'. This is supported by the academic and social progress which he made, as well as some significant progress in the area of independence. He particularly enjoyed the work and says that he felt that he was working at the right level. He especially enjoyed music and discovered a talent for playing the keyboard. He also enjoyed history, science and maths. He experienced some teasing from another autistic boy, which he didn't like, but says that the staff at the resource unit 'understood autism'. He was very happy there until 'things started to go wrong' in 2000.

Jordan experienced a traumatic personal loss in 2000 which is thought might have been the trigger for what he terms 'things going wrong.' As a result of this, he developed a heightened need, which has been termed 'an obsession' for friendships, but most particularly focused on a fixation with another student. Jordan describes his predominant feelings at this time as 'anxious and nervous'. Despite medication, Jordan's anxiety has continued to date and affects all of his life experiences. Jordan's anxiety and fixation at this time was severely impacting on all aspects of his life and it was clear that his needs and those of his family could no longer be met within mainstream. Because of this, the decision was made for him to attend a local special secondary school for children who had emotional and behavioural difficulties. This enabled Jordan to access residential provision for one or two nights a week.

Jordan describes the special school as 'like primary again'. He liked it there, but he 'learnt more in mainstream'. He was able to access a German class at a nearby comprehensive school, which he was found to have a talent for. He continued to feel anxious and nervous about relationships throughout this time and his level of anxiety and frustration was so high that he was often withdrawn from lessons and given alternative lunch time arrangements. Jordan sometimes self-harmed and required an extremely high level of support from two members of staff. Jordan's support needs increased to the point where that he was referred to a psychiatrist who specialized in ASC and his father was advised that a residential placement would be in his best interests. Jordan's father considered this and a placement at a residential college was sought.

In July 2003 it was recognized that it was not possible to find a placement in a residential college which suited Jordan's and his family's needs. The local special school considered that it was unable to continue to provide for Jordan's needs in its new Post-16 provision and a placement was hurriedly sought in the local mainstream Further Education college, which had an ASC specialist support team. The college recognized that they were not the ideal provider for Jordan, but agreed to provide an individual programme of supported learning which would be regularly monitored and reviewed.

Experience at college

Jordan wanted to go to mainstream college because he thought that he 'would have a good life there'. He explained that he didn't know what to expect but that he felt that his life would be good there because it was mainstream and he knew that this meant that he would learn more. He felt anxious about the move but felt confident because he already knew two members of the ASC support team who used to work at the resource unit. He enrolled onto a foundation level course in September 2003 without a formalized transition programme. Because of this, it was decided that the first term would effectively provide a period of transition for Jordan, as follows:

- Jordan would be provided with an individual induction period. The time allocated to this would be determined by Jordan's assessed needs.

- During the induction period, Jordan would receive one-to-one teaching from an experienced ASC specialist whom he was already familiar with.

- A taxi and one driver would be provided to transport Jordan to and from college for as long as his needs required it.

- Jordan would be escorted to and from college in the taxi, by the same member of staff who he worked with.

- Jordan would follow an individually planned programme of study which would familiarize him with the college environment and the people for two and a half days a week.

- Time at college would be gradually increased to enable Jordan to access mainstream classes, lecturers and time-tables.

- Jordan would have ASC-specific teaching in social skills.

- Jordan's progress would be reviewed every half term.

With intense support, Jordan was able to settle into college and progress well. Amazingly, by the end of the second week, he was confident enough to access some mainstream lessons with full support. This was gradually increased so that by the end of the first half term, all of Jordan's teaching took place alongside his tutor group. After the half term holiday, the second member of staff who Jordan was familiar with was introduced to work with Jordan and an extra day a week was added to his timetable. By the end of the first term, Jordan was attending the following lessons, with ASC specialist one-to-one support: English, Maths, Office Skills and IT.

Weekly social skills lessons were directed towards raising Jordan's self-esteem and confidence and minimizing his anxiety over friendships. This was done in a variety of ways, all of which were visual. I have already described growing a garden of friendships, in the previous chapter, which proved to be quite effective. Visual drawings of the brain were also used to enable Jordan to understand other people's thoughts and to enable him to manage his thinking about friendships and specific individuals. Jordan was also encouraged to develop interests in other areas to occupy his thoughts and provide occupation. As well as an interest in soap operas, he now has a particular interest in Spain and is also interested in the concept of God. He described his conversations with God to me as something which he is able to do in private, which makes him feel understood.

Jordan continued to progress throughout the year, with one-to-one ASC specialist support and at the end of the year was awarded certificates for the following:

- a Certificate of Achievement in Maths

- three Open College Credits in English at level 1

- OCR Certificate in text and word processing

- OCR Certificate in initial text processing

- a pass in four City and Guilds IT units.

Jordan is now accessing college at two different sites, for three half days and two full days a week. He is currently studying the following options at foundation level: English, Maths, Science, Business Studies, Spanish, Art and IT.

Jordan still receives transport to and from college, but this is now provided by two different taxi drivers and more than one escort who no longer sit in the back of the taxi or go to his front door to collect him. He continues to have one-to-one specialist support and social skills lessons once a week which he describes as having a set time to 'talk about my worries and something positive'. Jordan is now fully accessing a mainstream curriculum in a college which has an inclusive policy, with a number of other students who also have additional support needs. Most significantly for Jordan, in his second year of study he has made friendships with six or seven other students.

When Jordan first enrolled at college, there were a number of negative predictions and expectations of failure which have not materialized. It has been hard work and at times a huge struggle for Jordan and everyone who has supported him in his efforts to succeed on his terms. Jordan is rightly proud of his achievements and it is no wonder that he wants everyone to know about him and how well he has done.

Jordan's father Michael is keen that I should include his view that Jordan has only been able to do so well because of the high level of support which he has received throughout his life. Credit must also be given to him, for his perseverance in gaining a provision which has Jordan's needs at the centre. Jordan's account illustrates the importance and effectiveness of involving 'parents as partners' which has been advocated in this book. Out of college time, Jordan's needs are well supported by a local provider of services for autistic people, and the National Health psychiatric service. Michael is the pivot on which all Jordan's support balances and is currently the only link which joins up the different providers of services which Jordan receives. He has always ensured that communication channels are maintained and that there is no conflict of approach between the services.

Jordan has achieved in a way which has challenged even the most optimistic of us to re-evaluate our expectations of autistic people. It is now envisaged that he will be able to be supported towards more independent living in the future. This would have been thought impossible a short time ago. I hope that the will continue to 'have a good life there'.

Chris Fields

Chris writes poetry. He wrote this in 1998, when he was 19:

Love

Love is a knife, cutting through the skin of life.
Love is a dagger, stabbing you in the heart.
Love is a light, that lights up the dark.
Love is an eye, that looks out on the head of the world.

Love is a window on the house of earth sitting in the city called
the universe.
Love is a disease that eats your emotions and messes up your
life.
Love is a cure to a condition known as strife.
Love cheers me up when I am sad.
Love calms me down when I'm mad.
Love exists in me and you.
Love lasts for a life time or two.
Love loves me but does it love you?

I first met Chris and his mother in 2000, during the first year of my
appointment as Support Coordinator for autistic students at The
Sheffield College. Chris was quite unhappy at the time because he
had been at college for five years and he felt that his 'life was not
really progressing'. I have included his experience in this book for a
number of reasons: it is replicated in hundreds of instances throughout the country; it is not a thing of the past and young people still
experience similar negative attitudes and preconceptions, today; it
illustrates how ignorance and lack of knowledge of ASC, can lead to
low expectations and misrepresentations of a person's ability and
potential. However, despite all of this, it also illustrates the difference
which ASC specialist support can make to the experience of autistic
people in terms of achieving their dreams.

Background

Chris is intelligent and has Asperger syndrome, but as he was born
early in 1979, this was not recognized for many years. He is his parents' third child, and his mother confirms that he reached the
expected milestones for his age, up until the age of 20 months, when
he experienced a very obvious and severe reaction to the whooping
cough vaccine. This impacted hugely on his development and further
milestones were consequently delayed. Hearing tests at the age of
three confirmed that Chris had no hearing impairment, but as
language acquisition was delayed, he was referred for speech and
language therapy. The speech and language therapist possibly recognized some ASC-type behaviours and recommended referral to

Professor Elizabeth Newson in Nottingham. At this stage, Chris had a fascination with all things electrical and had some coordination difficulties, but autism was ruled out as he had good eye contact and was affectionate. Chris saw Professor Newson again, at the age of seven and at eleven, and then again at fifteen. It was at this stage that he was given a diagnosis of semantic pragmatic disorder and the term 'autism spectrum' was first used. This experience and type of diagnosis may seem unusual now but was not untypical at the time.

Chris attended a local state nursery school where he was extremely happy and formed a close relationship with his teacher which still exists, and then progressed to a small local primary school in the special schools sector where his needs were understood and he felt secure and was very happy. The school attempted integration with a mainstream school for one day a week, but this was unsuccessful. When Chris was in Year 6, it was clear that his educational needs would not be met in the special school secondary sector, and the only alternative choice available to him was integration into the local comprehensive school, with generic support. With only 800 pupils, the comprehensive school was comparatively small, but still extremely confusing and unsuitable for Chris.

Chris' secondary school experience was 'awful'. He received minimal support which was inadequate and did not address his ASC-specific needs. Most of the teachers did not demonstrate a desire to understand or address his needs in their teaching methods and despite being intelligent, Chris was not able to achieve in line with his potential, in any area of the curriculum, with the exception of Science. Like most children who have Asperger syndrome, Chris was subtly bullied and this was not effectively addressed by the school. Typically, lunchtimes were particularly difficult as was the boys' PE changing room. Two or three of the teachers were kind to him, but he was unhappy for most of this time and his mother received frequent phone calls from the school. Chris' parents attempted to work with the school in meeting his needs, but were met with negative stereotyping and preconceptions. In the absence of any effective support, Chris' mother provided the school with the following hand-written guidelines:

Areas which may cause concern

Having to rush.

Being uncertain what is required.

Being uncertain where he needs to go.

Breaks, lunch time etc.

Keeping his possessions organized.

Feeling lonely and anxious about the way people look at him.

Sometimes talks to himself.

Needs (like all of us) reassurance and praise.

Travelling alone.

Despite this, the secondary school experience can be described as 'disastrous'. The school's lack of understanding and negativity was further demonstrated by their recommendation for residential Post-16 provision. Chris' parents considered this option and after visiting a number of residential provisions recognized that they had been misguided as the provisions were clearly unsuitable for someone of Chris' intelligence, ability and potential. Chris left school in July 1994 with two D grades in GCSE Science (Dual award).

Experience at college

Chris enrolled at the local FE college in September 1995, somewhat ironically at the time when the Education Authority opened an Integrated Resource Unit for children with 'severe communication disorders' in the comprehensive school which he left.

Chris is a friendly, quiet person who is very well mannered and polite. He does not display what might be termed 'challenging behaviours' and as a result when he was at college, was given minimal generic support. Chris' need for structure and organizational support was not met by the FE ethos of 'independent learning' and as his condition was not understood, his academic ability and potential was not recognized at this time. He was generally 'allowed to get on as he wanted' and was not stretched in any way. Chris had a talent for IT and as he did not have sufficient academic qualifications studied this at Foundation level. He was successful in achieving a pass in this by the end of his first year at college but did not feel academically stretched. Socially, college was less problematic than school and Chris made friendships during this year, one of which continues.

The failure to recognize Chris' potential together with the lack of provision of structure and organizational support led to increased social opportunities at the expense of academic learning. This in turn encouraged the continuation of low expectations which concealed Chris' potential further. The result of this was that in subsequent years, Chris was directed to a variety of courses which did not address his skills or abilities and only vaguely reflected his hobby interests. This can be seen in the following summary of his achievements:

Summary

1994–1995: Chris gained a pass in GNVQ IT at Foundation level.

1995–1996: Chris gained a pass in GNVQ Art and Design at Foundation level.

1996–1997: Chris gained Foundation level OCN Credits in Cookery, Leisure and Recreation. He also achieved a Grade E in GCSE IT.

1997–1998: Chris gained a Grade D in GCSE Drama.

1998–1999: Chris gained a DOVE pass in Performing Arts.

1999–2000: Chris successfully completed a number of units in Vocational Music.

Towards the end of the academic year 1999 to 2000, it was thought that Chris had exhausted all options which were available to him. He was unfulfilled and unhappy and his parents did not know where to turn for help. In desperation, his mother approached the Integrated Resource Unit at Chris' old school to learn that they were now partners in providing a Post-16 ASC-specific support provision at the college. Chris was referred to this service for support.

When I first met Chris at the end of this year, it was obvious that he was unhappy. He told me that he felt that his life was not progressing and I will never forget his answer when I asked him how he would like it to progress: he told me that he would like to go to university. I asked his reasons for this and he told me that he wanted to follow in his brother and sister's footsteps. He said that this was his dream and that he felt that he could achieve it if he studied computing. We discussed the barriers to him accessing university and Chris was clear that neither his ability nor his autism presented insurmountable barriers to this, but that his lack of academic qualifications did. Chris wanted to break down those barriers and gain the entry requirements for university. At this point I was uncertain if this was a realistic option for Chris, but decided to work with him in realizing his dream on the basis that time would clarify its appropriateness. I was aware that this was a risk, but thought that time and experience would provide the basis for 'counselling him out' of his decision, if it was inappropriate.

As Chris was now 21, it was possible to consider the less traditional route of an adult Access to Higher Education course. Chris expressed the need for a fresh start which would enable him to leave the negative experiences of the previous four years behind him and this was made possible because the college operated on a number of different sites. The lateness of Chris' application however, meant that there was not a place available on the two-year IT Access Course in the centre of his choice, so an alternative had to be sought. In September 2000, Chris enrolled on an individual 'mix and match' programme of study at his second choice centre, which involved travelling across the city. This required learning self-travelling skills, but enabled Chris to study a variety of City and Guilds IT modules whilst also studying the Open College Network (OCN) Maths and English at level 2, which were accepted by the universities as GCSE equivalents.

Chris was initially given 100 per cent support from the autism specialist support team at college but it was quickly realized that he could be independent in three of his IT lessons. One-to-one specialist in-class support was provided in all other areas throughout the year. Chris found the change to a higher level of study satisfying in terms of realizing his potential, but also stressful in terms of the workload and the challenges which it presented. The effort of processing information for study, together with the extra travelling time often left him exhausted and the new concept of homework impacted significantly on his home time and family relationships. To accommodate this, homework tutorials were provided in English and Maths, with additional e-mail support in English and close contact was maintained with his parents. It was not an easy year for Chris, but as the year progressed, his confidence grew and he successfully completed a period of work experience and passed all modules at the end of the academic year. This enabled him to progress in 2001 on to the second year of the Access Course in his preferred college centre, which was also closer to home. As well as providing a foundation for further progress, this experience enabled Chris to develop socially. During this time, he was introduced to another student who had a diagnosis of Asperger syndrome who had similar interests and experience at college and a lasting friendship developed.

I asked Chris to rate his personal satisfaction and happiness levels for the time when I first met him, on a scale of 1 to 10. He rated them both as 4. I asked how he would rate these levels now, and he rated them both at 9. I asked him if these levels had been higher at any time and they were at their highest during the academic year 2001 to 2002, when he was on the Access Course. When I asked what the deciding factors were in these ratings he was clear that they were directly linked to the level of work and the level of support.

The Access Course was very satisfying for Chris, on a number of levels. As he indicated, the work and support which he received were at the right level for him so that he felt intellectually stretched without feeling that he was drowning in work, but the contribution of the group, in terms of its composition and dynamics was also significant. For the first time, Chris was studying with a group of mature people who had similar interests to him, who recognized his needs and his ability and treated him as an equal. This environment was fulfilling and rewarding for Chris. During this time, he made another lasting friendship with a student who was studying in the same department, but on a different IT course.

Chris successfully completed the Access Course in the summer of 2002 and applied for admission to one of the local universities to study Computer Programming. Chris and the autism support team had the benefit of knowledge gained from his friend's experience of study at this university and it became clear that it was not a suitable place for Chris to study because:

1.   there would be insufficient support

2.   the type of support available would not address Chris' ASC-specific needs.

Chris was given the alternative option of studying computer programming part time on an Higher National Diploma (HND) course, within the college. This would involve some evening study at yet another college centre, but would guarantee the continuation of ASC specialist support. There was also an option of continuing study for a further year, on completion of the HND, to convert the qualification into a BSc. Chris decided to accept this option and enrolled on the HND in Computer Programming in September 2002.

Studying at his pace with support has enabled Chris to achieve four merits and five or six passes to date and he is expected to complete his HND in June of this year (2005). It has been a long and challenging journey for him and at times he has found the work very pressurized. In addition, each stage has brought changes and the requirement for new skills which Chris has had to learn, alongside his academic learning. His achievements have been phenomenal, but only possible because he has been fully supported at home by his parents who are the only people who see the full extent of the pressures and frustration which he experiences. I asked Chris why his experience on the HND course was slightly less positive than his experience on the Access Course and his comments were that in the beginning it was 'absolutely fabulous' but over the last year, his support has been inconsistent due to staff illness which has not been possible to cover. When I asked him if anything could have been improved, his answer was that the quality of his support was 'ten out of ten' but that cover should be provided for the person who was sick.

I was concerned that Chris might be disappointed because he had not gone to university. He assured me that he is not, as he feels that the option of a BSc is still open to him if he chooses. He has however, decided that his next challenge is employment and he would like to become a CISCO Certified Network Administrator. He intends to enrol on another part-time course to qualify him for this and I am sure that he will be successful.

Chris is particularly close to his older sister and her husband and has written the following humorous poem about his brother-in-law:

The Kite Surfer

My Brother in Law
Who lives far away
Goes to work everyday.
But now and again
To get away from the strain
From his job
He does his hobby.

Normal people do Gardening,
Others may go out,
Some may even surf the Internet.
My Brother in Law surfs the way
Oh you say he's a surfer.
He's tried it and didn't like it.
No he likes to ride the waves and the wind.
And he may do a bit of Windsurfing.
But he mostly goes extreme

This hobby is dangerous,
This hobby is not for the normal
This hobby is Kite surfing.
He starts off in the water
Cruising off at 15 mph,
Then a gust of wind hits his kite,
Whoosh, he takes off 15 ft into the air,
Time shuts down,
He feels the wind through his hair,
He sees the world from the sky,
Adrenaline rushing through his veins,
Time goes back to normal,
Splash, he hits the water,
Waves hit him and he feels good.

Yes, This sport is not for the normal
This sport is extreme.
This sport is for the extreme sportsman.
This sport is not recommended for normal people.
But this is my brother in law and
Dentistry is a boring job
So he needs a break sometime.
My brother in law, The Kite Surfer.

Edward Harries

Edward is one of the most determined and highly motivated people I know. He has a huge personality. He also has 'classic autism' which impacts significantly on his learning and masks his intelligence. I have included his account because he has been my inspiration during the ten years that I have known him. Edward doesn't 'struggle' with his autism or with life. He wants to succeed and he has joyfully bull-dozed through all the barriers which might have prevented him from doing so. He has taught me more about autism than all the books I have read and he has challenged and continues to challenge my pre-conceptions as well as my skills. Edward is the example that proves that inclusion is not only for those autistic people who are labelled as having Asperger syndrome. Inclusion is for all.

I have been able to include a great deal of extra information in this account, thanks to the meticulous recording of Edward's parents, who in refusing to accept the advice which they were given by some professionals set the pattern for an 'Edward-centred' approach.

Background

It was never confirmed but Edward's parents take the view that his autism is the result of a long labour and a forceps delivery, during which he possibly experienced oxygen starvation. He is his parents' second child and his mother describes him as a restless baby who was smiley and photogenic but slept little. By the time he was a year old, Edward's parents were aware that his play patterns were repetitive and that if he was focused on something, he appeared not to hear. By the age of 18 months, this was beginning to concern them as was his apparent lack of language development. They began to observe him more closely and he was referred for hearing tests, just after his two-year medical, as a consequence. The test results confirmed that Edward had 'perfect hearing' so he was referred for speech therapy in May 1986.

In September 1986, Edward was referred for multidisciplinary assessment to the local National Health Service children's centre, which specializes in assessing children who have neurobiological conditions which affect their development. He took part in a three-day assessment which involved full psychological testing, tests on language development, a play assessment and observations on the mother–child relationship. At the end of these, his parents were told that Edward had a 'communication disorder with inflexibility of play and poor socialization'. They found this diagnosis unsatisfactory as it did not provide them with any guidance which would enable them to assist Edward, so his parents requested a more specific diagnosis which the authority were reluctant to give and which they felt related to the policy of 'not labelling' which was relatively common at the time. They were told that Edward 'might never speak' and that he should have 'secure residential educational provision'. They were also told to 'give him lots of love'.

Edward's parents are intelligent, well-educated people who wanted practical guidance which would enable them to do what was best for their child. Apart from the practical support which they were given from the speech therapist, they were given little advice, information or practical guidance to enable them to do this. They had suspected that Edward was autistic and their thoughts were confirmed around this time, by reading a magazine article. As a result of this, they contacted the National Autistic Society for more information, but the information which they received, (which they still have) was 'very depressing'. It brought the realization that there would be no external agency which would provide the type of support and guidance which they wanted and also contributed to a sense of anger that Edward was being 'written off'. Edward's mother explains that she 'didn't accept what she was told' and this made her subject to negative criticism from some professionals at the time. Her subsequent reaction was driven by her own background in skills development within employment, and she 'sat back and thought about what would prevent Edward from learning'. Edward's older brother started nursery around this time and this gave her the opportunity to work alone with Edward. She focused first of all on 'encouraging him to participate in what was going on around him' and then on the 'underpinning skills for learning'. 'Edward's Book' from October 1987, when he was three and a half, records the following learning experiences:

- picture recognition
- naming
- visual games such as 'snap' and picture matching
- making pictures
- identifying parts of the body
- potato printing and naming
- using sticky shapes to make a picture
- guided computer experience
- encouraging talking
- jigsaws.

The same book records Edward's progress. So that by the age of about four Edward was:

- starting to learn basic 'turn taking' during board games
- starting first stage writing and number exercises using the Ladybird series
- counting up to 10 and showing recognition of most numbers up to 10, by pointing
- using flash cards to name items
- recognizing some items in written form only
- developing understanding of some letter sounds
- identifying the primary colours, sometimes with prompting

- understanding concepts like day and night; hot and cold; up and down, big and little etc.

- answering questions about a picture often using pointing to give the answer of 'where'

- using the questions 'where?' and 'can I?' but not 'why?' or 'how?'

In addition, Edward's language was developing so that:

> He has a wide vocabulary and now uses a range of short sentences, which he puts together himself. Relies much less on copying to produce language, but if he can avoid using structured language he will.
>
> Comprehends a wide range of spoken language but may need things repeated if there are several points to remember all in one sentence, or where the natural situation is unfamiliar. (Edward's Book, 1987)

At the same time, Edward accessed all activities which were suitable for someone his age, such as 'Tumble Tots' and the local playgroup. The playgroup was unable to provide the structured activities which Edward needed so at the age of four, he attended a Montessori nursery. Both of these placements were advised by an assessment teacher who was linked to the children's centre where Edward had been assessed. Edward was happy at nursery and remained there until after the age when he would normally have attended school. During this time, Edward was accepted into the rising 5 class at his local infant school, but the head teacher did not think that the school would be able to cater for his needs on a full-time basis, so his parents contacted the Local Education Authority (LEA) who initiated the process of Statementing for Special Educational Needs. Recommendations were made at this point by the speech therapist and an educational psychologist that Edward should be placed in a school where speech therapy was integral to the learning but the list of special schools which the LEA gave to Edward's parents for them to visit, included those for children with behavioural difficulties, some of which were located out of the city. The suggestion was made that an out of city placement might be in Edward's best interests. Edward and his mother visited and assessed the schools suggested by the LEA and found them to be inappropriate, so once again Edward's parents made the decision not to follow the advice which they were given. This made them vulnerable to further negative criticism from some professionals who thought that they had unreasonably high expectations for their child and were perhaps pushing him in order to satisfy their own needs.

Edward's parents recognized that they would have to be proactive in achieving what was best for their son and visited a small local special primary school which was coincidentally close to where they lived and which provided communication therapy. The head teacher was 'positive, open and flexible' and agreed to accept Edward with the condition that the LEA provide additional support which would enable the school to fully address his needs. He was also willing to liaise with the head teacher of the local mainstream infant school to enable Edward to access integrated provision for one day a week. Having negotiated with both head teachers who were agreeable to this proposal, Edward's parents then approached the LEA with what was in effect their preferred choice of an individual, person-centred provision for their son, and requested that the LEA provide additional support to meet Edward's needs. The LEA provided this in line with the Statement of Special Educational Needs, which was eventually altered to acknowledge that Edward was autistic.

Edward was extremely happy at primary school, and this has persisted throughout most of his educational experiences. His reading skills continued to develop well although Maths presented significant challenges, but the most positive aspect of Edward's education at this stage was the provision of communication therapy. Edward had developed some language skills, and the communication therapy encouraged the further development of these and also of wider communication skills. In addition, it enabled him to become more willing to accept input from others. Alongside of this, the mainstream integration worked well and provided interactions with mainstream peers which formed a solid basis for future integration.

By this time, Edward's mother was a member of the board of governors at the school and the governors, together with the head teacher, a group of parents and some education officers began to address the lack of integrated provision at secondary level for autistic pupils. As a result, in 1994, when Edward was in Year 5, the authority, after much negotiation, opened its first Integrated Resource Unit, for secondary age pupils with 'severe communication disorders', attached to Edward's local mainstream comprehensive school. The development of this is well documented in *Access and Inclusion for Children with Autistic Spectrum Disorders* (Hesmondhalgh and Breakey 2001).

I first met Edward at his primary school in the summer of 1995. At school, most of his language was echolaic, but despite this he was learning French in preparation for secondary school. I accompanied him with two other pupils to a communication therapy session and the high level of his support needs was obvious. I privately questioned the suitability of integration for Edward as he has 'classic' autism and at that time displayed all the 'typical' behaviours which are associated with the condition. The contrast between the small safe special primary school and the large 'typical' comprehensive school was evident, as was the clash that this would make with Edward's autism. When Edward started at the comprehensive school, his determination to push back any boundaries which prevented him from participating fully in the experience quickly answered my questions and doubts and Edward thrived in the environment. However, Edward's mother confirms that she and his father were aware that this was 'a gamble' for him. Their conviction to 'give him a chance' was guided by their knowledge of him and his sheer determination to succeed.

With the exception of Religious Education, History and Geography, which provided teaching time for the 'hidden curriculum', Edward was fully integrated into the Year 7 curriculum with 100 per cent one-to-one ASC-specific support from the most skilled of the ASC support team. He was never unhappy and had to be persuaded not to go to school on the few occasions when he was ill. He thrived academically and socially and his language development progressed so that he became able to express himself without using phrases from his favourite television programmes. Supporting Edward was not a job for the faint-hearted as he pushed the boundaries, challenged the assumptions and stretched the skills of everyone who worked with him. Responding positively to this was only made possible by daily communication with Edward's parents which as well as maintaining an effective working partnership, provided advice and guidelines on how to effectively communicate with and support him.

Against all the odds and with some trepidation on behalf of the support team, Edward embarked in Year 9 on a supported integration into work programme in the offices of a large national insurance company, which also entailed some independent travelling on public transport. This was so successful that it lasted for three years and provided a skills base for further educational opportunities for Edward. Edward left school in July 2000, extremely confident and with the following academic qualifications:

GCSE Art and Design: Grade D
GCSE Food Technology: Grade E
GCSE Maths: Grade F
GCSE IT: Grade F
Certificate of Attendance in English: Pass.

Experience at college

Edward attended for interview at college during the summer of 2000 in the middle of an inspection. He is six foot tall and well built and looked impressive in his suit, shirt and tie. He took the situation very seriously and arrived, complete with clipboard and pen which added to the overall impression of officiousness. He waited, standing upright, with pen in hand, in the Student Support Services waiting area for me and the course coordinator who was interviewing him, to arrive. When I arrived, I was surprised that the course coordinator was wearing his cycling clothes and was aware that there had been some cause for merriment. After a successful interview, which resulted in Edward's acceptance onto the Foundation level programme, it was explained to me that the person interviewing Edward had cycled into work without picking up the bag which contained his work clothes and that he was hoping to conceal this from the inspectors whilst his appropriate clothes were being delivered by a family member. As he arrived to apologize and explain his appearance to Edward and his mother, he mistook Edward, standing tall, complete with clipboard for an inspector. I wish I had been there to see his reaction!

Edward took to college like a 'duck to water' and was blissfully oblivious of all the preparation work which had taken place to ensure a successful transition for him. The Foundation level course which he was studying took place at all of the five college centres and it was expected that students should study at the one which was nearest to their home. For Edward, this meant that he had the choice of two centres, both of which were the least autism friendly of all the centres. Extensive negotiations had to take place to justify the exceptional circumstances which required that Edward travel across the city to the centre which was furthest away from his home, but would provide the most suitable learning environment for his autism-specific needs. In addition, as all of Edward's schooling had taken place within walking distance of his home, the local authority had never provided transport assistance. The provision of this at college, also required justification and negotiation. The link between the Integrated Resource Unit and the autism support team at college assisted the organization of introductory visits so it was possible to familiarize Edward with the college environment well in advance, whilst extensive but subtle discussions took place to identify a personal tutor and teaching staff who were flexible enough to accommodate Edward's needs. These people were provided with a student profile which outlined all of Edward's needs and gave advice and guidance for accommodating them. It was also recognized that support should initially be provided only by the most experienced and skilled members of the support team who Edward was already familiar with and that other members of the team should receive 'on the job' training from these people, which would extend their skills and Edward's support base. Edward then received one-to-one support of the type which is described throughout this book. Within this framework, Edward thrived socially, academically and his confidence 'knew no bounds'.

Edward spent two years studying at Foundation level where as well as gaining double the number of credits which were necessary for progression to higher level courses, he extended the skills which underpin learning. In particular, he developed flexibility and became more able to compromise in terms of presenting his work in formats which were required for accreditation. He also began to understand the concept of 'a first draft' and developed the ability to complete projects over a period of time, neither of which was initially within his reach. Edward also continued to develop his independence skills so that at the end of the second year, he had the choice of studying either Art and Design or IT at Intermediate level. The decision was difficult and after considerable discussions with his parents, Edward decided that even though IT might present the possibility of employment opportunities, he wanted to study Art and Design for his enjoyment.

The academic year 2002 to 2003 was the most successful for Edward in terms of his academic achievement, self-satisfaction and social progression. He excelled at Art and Design and loved the relationships which he had with his support staff. Edward has always loved attractive young women and he became especially fond of one of his LSAs. Life drawing presented a particular challenge for his support workers, but using a video as part of preparation, both at college and at home, helped to overcome any concerns which they had and Edward approached the task with maturity, confidence and professionalism. Edward has always been popular with his mainstream peers, but his approach to his art, earned him their respect and admiration.

By this time, Edward was fully independent at lunch times and by the summer term had taken the opportunity to develop friendships with a group of young male students who were studying sport at an advanced level. He delighted in 'hanging out with the lads' and they welcomed his company which provided additional opportunities for him to chat to some of the most attractive girls in the college. He blossomed in this environment and at the end of the year his final display compared favourably in quality with his peers and far exceeded theirs in terms of output. He successfully achieved a Merit in Intermediate GNVQ Art and Design and was very proud of his achievement. Edward remembers this time as one of 'happy memories'.

The academic year 2003 to 2004 was far more difficult for Edward and retrospect is a far better tool than prediction for identifying potential problems. In retrospect, Edward's progress and determination to succeed was so successful that it effectively concealed the severity of his autism and everyone underestimated the effect that change would have on him.

Edward's parents were advised that he had probably reached his highest level of academic achievement in Art and Design, and this influenced his decision to follow a course, which would enable him to use his IT skills and attract potential employment opportunities. In the absence of a suitable IT course, Edward was guided towards an Office Technology and Administration course, which in retrospect was probably not the right course for him. This entailed a move of centre for Edward to a small 'autism friendly' centre, where problems were not anticipated. In retrospect, no one recognized that there would be a lack of opportunity for Edward to develop social relationships at this new centre, and as Edward's new-found friends had moved on to study at university, the effect of their absence was not recognized. At the time, no one fully understood the significance of these friendships to Edward, or the impact which they had made to his personal recognition of his success, confidence and self-esteem. The consequence of this soon became evident as Edward was not happy in his new learning environment.

For the first time, Edward was not joyful in his studies. The nature of the course meant that teaching staff were not as flexible as in Art and Design and Edward's expectations based on his experience of the previous year were not met. He was no longer supported by his favourite LSA, the impact of which was quickly recognized and addressed, but it was an extremely difficult year for him during which he had to confront some issues which were painful for him and those who supported him. The gender and racial balance of his peer group made it impossible for Edward to develop any satisfying relationships and he blamed himself for this. He felt that people didn't understand him and was confronted with the very painful fact that his communication skills did not enable him to attract the type of girls that he wanted. Edward felt this acutely and despite attempts to address it, believed that he must have done something wrong.

The positive aspect of this year for Edward was that it provided him with a supported work experience placement in the office of the Sheffield Royal Society for the Blind which is something which he enjoys greatly and has been able to continue as a volunteer. He was also successful in gaining his level one qualification.

The college management was unable at this point to suggest a way forward which was satisfactory for Edward and he struggled with these issues over the summer holiday period so that he felt unable to contemplate returning to college full time. He is currently studying computing, for half a day a week in one of the college's community centres, which he says does not stretch his skills but which he is enjoying.

These personal issues also coincided with a planned move to supported independent living which Edward had wanted since his older brother left home for university. Edward's parents judged that he needed to focus on this for the time being and he successfully moved into his new accommodation two weeks ago. I visited him today and he was extremely confident, proud and happy of this new achievement. I am certain that he will rise to this new challenge in his characteristically determined way.

References

Abercrombie, D. (1968) 'Paralanguage.' *British Journal of Disorders of Communication* 3, 55–59.

Attwood, T. (1998) *Asperger's Syndrome. A Guide for Parents and Professionals.* London: Jessica Kingsley Publishers.

Barnard, J., Harvey, V., Prior, A. and Potter, D. (2000) *Inclusion and autism: is it working?* London: The National Autistic Society.

Barnard, J., Harvey, V., Prior, A. and Potter, D. (2001) *Ignored or ineligible: the reality for adults with autistic spectrum disorders.* London: The National Autistic Society.

Barnard, J., Broach, S., Potter, D., and Prior, A. (2002) *Autism in schools: crisis or challenge?* London: The National Autistic Society.

Barnes, C. (2003) 'What a difference a decade makes: reflections on doing "emancipatory" disability research.' *Disability and Society 18*, 1, 3–17.

Baron-Cohen, S. (2000) 'Theory of mind and autism: a fifteen year review.' In S. Baron-Cohen, H. Tager-Flushberg and D.J. Cohen (eds) *Understanding Other Minds: Perspectives from Developmental Cognitive Neuroscience.* Oxford: Oxford University Press.

Baron-Cohen, S. (2003) *The Essential Difference.* London: Penguin Books.

Baron-Cohen, S., Leslie, A.M. and Frith, U. (1985) 'Does the autistic child have a theory of mind?' *Cognition 21*, 37–46.

Centre for Studies on Inclusive Education (CSIE) *Inclusive Education – A Framework for Change.* http://inclusion.uwe.ac.uk/csie/framewrk.htm (accessed 20.03.00).

Centre for Studies on Inclusive Education (CSIE) *Inclusive Further Education.* http://inclusion.uwe.ac.uk/csie/tmlnsn.htm. (accessed 20.03.00).

Copeland, J. (1972) *For the Love of Ann.* London: Arrow Books.

Curran, J. P. and Monti, P.M. (1982) *Social Skills Training: A Practical Handbook for Assessment and Treatment.* New York, NY: Guilford.

Frith, U. (1989) *Autism: Explaining the Enigma.* Oxford: Blackwell.

Grandin T. and Scariano, M. (1986) *Emergence Labelled Autistic.* Location: Costelle.

Gray, C. (1994) *Comic Strip Conversations.* Arlington: Future Horizons.

Happé, F. (1999) 'Autism: cognitive deficit or cognitive style?' *Trends in Cognitive Sciences 3*, 216–222.

Hesmondhalgh, M. and Breakey, C. (2001) *Access and Inclusion for Children with Autistic Spectrum Disorders: 'Let Me In'.* London: Jessica Kingsley Publishers.

Jackson, L. (2002) *Freaks, Geeks and Asperger Syndrome: A User Guide to Adolescence.* London: Jessica Kingsley Publishers.

Jordan, R. and Powell, S. (eds) (1997) *Autism and Learning: A Guide to Good Practice.* London: David Fulton Publishers.

Lawson, W. (2001) *Understanding and Working with the Spectrum of Autism: An Insider's View.* London: Jessica Kingsley Publishers.

Matson, J.L. and Ollendick, T.H. (1988) *Enhancing Children's Social Skills.* New York: Pergamon Press.

National Autistic Society (1993, revised in 2003) *Approaches to Autism.* London: NAS.

Piaget, J. (1952) *The Origins of Intelligence in Children.* New York: International Universities Press.

Sinclair, J. (1993) 'Don't Mourn for Us.' *Our Voice 1,* 3.

Tarleton, B. (2004) 'Disability Discrimination Act: taking the work forward. Research and development projects 2003/5. Project 19: Developing inclusive provision for learners with autistic spectrum disorders.' London: Learning and Skills Development Agency. (http://www.lsneducation.org.uk/dda/files/projectreports/PLR19.doc)

Willey, L.H. (1999) *Pretending to be Normal: Living with Asperger's Syndrome.* London: Jessica Kingsley Publishers.

Williams, D. (1996) *Autism: An Inside-Out Approach.* London: Jessica Kingsley Publishers.

Williams, D. (1998) *Nobody Nowhere: The Remarkable Autobiography of an Autistic Girl.* London: Jessica Kingsley Publishers.

Williams, D. (1998) *Somebody Somewhere: Breaking Free from the World of Autism.* London: Jessica Kingsley Publishers.

Index